KU-541-573

# LEADERSHIP EXPLOSION

# LEADERSHIP EXPLOSION

**Philip King**

**HODDER AND STOUGHTON**
LONDON SYDNEY AUCKLAND TORONTO

**British Library Cataloguing in Publication Data**

King, Philip
    Leadership explosion. – (Hodder Christian
    paperbacks).
    1. Christian leadership
    I. Title
    248.4        BV652.1

    ISBN 0 340 39991 0

*Copyright © 1987 by Philip King. First printed 1987. All rights reserved.
No part of this publication may be reproduced or transmitted in any form or
by any means, electronically or mechanically, including photocopying,
recording or any information storage or retrieval system, without either the
prior permission in writing from the publisher or a licence, permitting
restricted copying, issued by the Copyright Licensing Agency, 33–34 Alfred
Place, London WC1E 7DP. Printed in Great Britain for Hodder &
Stoughton Limited, Mill Road, Dunton Green, Sevenoaks, Kent by Cox &
Wyman Limited, Reading, Berks. Photoset by Rowland Phototypesetting
Limited, Bury St Edmunds, Suffolk. Hodder & Stoughton Editorial
Office: 47 Bedford Square, London WC1B 3DP.*

# CONTENTS

# FOREWORD

When I was an Area Dean in London, the Deanery Synod was stunned into silence one evening when we were discussing 'continuing ministerial education'. Two of the clergymen present exploded with rage, declared to us all that they were the educators and needed no further education and then stormed out of the hall. Of course, they were exceptions – or were they? We may not 'explode' but we can all be self-protective of our leadership and so resent criticism or suggestions or comment or even further training.

So Philip King's thorough examination of leadership ought to be read by all leaders with humility and openness. It should also be the basis for a series of constructive discussions in churches and for a possible reappraisal of aspects of the church's leadership. This book will stimulate, annoy, enlighten, hurt, clarify, correct and widen our thinking – not necessarily in that order! One invaluable ingredient is the world-wide dimension of the author's thinking – drawing on his first-hand experiences in other parts of the world as well as in Britain, and this clearly enriches the insights given.

Amongst the many good things in the book there stands out for me the *strategy* of leadership as something to be thought through, worked at and adjusted; the *sharing* of leadership as vital to church growth though without abdicating overall leadership (and sharing involves training thoroughly, which is often the role of what Philip King calls 'super churches' in training for service in many other places); the *sensitivity* of leadership in adapting to a situation, in listening and thinking what is right rather than imposing a personal style; and lastly, the *servanthood* of leadership as a foil to personal ego-trips (when I became a Bishop I carried a towel in my pocket to remind me of the servant's role of the upper room).

Philip King has done a splendid job in putting his examination of leadership so fully and clearly. May the book result in more effective leadership in our churches and so greater fruit to the glory of the leader of the Church, Jesus Christ our Lord.

Michael Baughen
Bishop of Chester

# INTRODUCTION

'I keep committee meetings brief. Most members know very little about the subjects being discussed.' The speaker was an experienced minister of an older generation, leading a suburban church packed with professional people. He clearly found committee meetings a waste of time and presumably the members did too. I came away with a number of questions. Did his committee members really know nothing about the subjects being discussed? Most of them were skilled and articulate in the business world; had the church failed to train them in its world? Did the fault lie with the agenda, or had there been a refusal to share leadership? Had the minister ever been trained to share?

Styles of leadership is one of the burning issues in the church today. I have had the privilege of visiting a large number of churches, not only in Great Britain and Ireland, but also in Latin America, North America, Africa and Australia. I have encountered on many occasions a happy partnership between minister and people, but in other cases I have found church members frustrated. At one extreme there has been an authoritarian leadership which has never learnt to share and at the other there has been no leadership and no clearly communicated vision. Some never delegate, others tend to abdicate. My own questions started several years ago when I moved from a suburban to an inner city church. In suburbia committee meetings had the atmosphere of the House of Commons; top-flight business executives came armed with sheaves of paper and delivered forceful, cogent speeches. A strong lead was needed from the chairman. In some suburban churches committees can become a theatre of war; 'I go into the room like a general going into a staff meeting on the eve of battle,' said one minister. In the inner city it quickly became apparent that any decision could be pushed through with ease. Members were used to taking orders, not giving them and felt uncomfortable at being asked for an opinion, let alone a decision. An attitude of dependence at work had been reinforced in society and in the church. I had to develop a 'hands off' style of leadership in order to encourage others to pray, discuss and decide. I have visited other inner city churches, however, where there are heated debates, dominated by trade union and other local leaders.

Looking at leadership styles inevitably raises a host of questions. What are the expectations of leadership in different contexts and cultures? Is there a blueprint for leadership in the New Testament? Is there just one right style of leadership or can it vary from person to person and from place to place? The aim of this book is not to record the pronouncements of an 'expert', not to provide slick, umbrella answers but to ask the right questions so that the answers can be worked at and worked out in each local church. Part I describes the theories and styles of Christian leadership drawn from sociology, from different cultures and from scripture. Part II deals with the practice of leadership, and the Appendix suggests some practical projects. Scripture references are from the New International Version unless otherwise stated. I hope it will be of value not only to professional leaders – clergy, pastors and ministers – but also to those who are called to give a lead in youth clubs, Sunday schools and in house groups.

The number of books on leadership is increasing. Some are devotional and inspirational, while others draw on the world of business management techniques. There is a place for a book which looks both at scripture and at management theory in order to work out guidelines for the local and the wider church. I have called it *Leadership Explosion* because one of the greatest needs in the church and in the world today is the multiplication of effective Christian leaders. The effective leader learns to recognise and develop the gifts of others and share leadership with them.

I have decided to keep most of my illustrations anonymous as it is far from easy to give a balanced account in a short space and many local church structures are evolving and changing; what is true one year may not be true the next. I am grateful to the South American Missionary Society for the grant of study leave for research and writing, to Doris Hunt for the final typing and to my colleagues and my family for their patience. I am indebted to a large number of churches and individuals for material and advice and without committing them to an endorsement of what follows I should like to thank especially Gervais Angel, Josephine Bax, Mark Birchall, Martin Goldsmith, Tony Tyndale and David Wasdell.

Philip King

# Part I

# Theories and Styles of Leadership

# 1 DICTATOR, BUREAUCRAT OR COUNSELLOR?

## Sociology and Christian leadership

What do sociologists have to say about styles of leadership?

The different management approaches.

Is there one right style or approach?

Questions of management affect every institution, sacred or secular. The head teacher of a school has to divide his time between administration, staff and pupils. During an industrial crisis he will be forced to spend several hours in negotiating with teachers' unions. If he is head of a large comprehensive he may have difficulty in limiting the time spent on administration in order to keep his hand in on teaching. Both head teachers and senior nursing officers complain that they become overloaded with paper and have less and less time for people. The flow of paper is increased because we live in a day of research and analysis and one of the aspects of life in industry, education and the health service is a continuing evaluation of management styles and structures. Sociologists have an important contribution to make in this analysis and because the church is a human institution as well as a divine one the insights of sociology can be valuable in understanding how it operates. Christian leaders usually assume that their style of leadership is rooted in theological convictions. It may well be, but their convictions and their choice of style may be influenced by history and by the pattern of organisation in society at large. For example, the organisation of the Church of England has been shaped and reshaped by different periods of history and at some points still retains vestiges of feudal society. When a vicar goes to a new parish he undergoes a ceremony called an 'induction'. He lays a hand on the doorknob of the parish church and tolls the bell as a sign of taking freehold possession. He kneels before the bishop and takes oaths of allegiance that are reminiscent of a medieval vassal swearing allegiance to his lord. This is not to suggest that patterns of church organisation or theological convictions are merely reactions to historical, social or psychological factors, but simply that the social sciences can help to lay bare our assumptions, clarify our choices and bring us back to scripture in a fresh way with new questions and a greater openness.

In 1947 the sociologist Max Weber described three types of leadership in society – the 'traditional', the 'charismatic' and the 'bureaucratic'.[1] In subsequent years sociologists identified two other styles – 'human relations' and 'organic' or 'systemic'. In 1968 Dr Peter Rudge used sociological theory to categorise styles of leadership in the church. His book *Ministry and Management* uses the categories mentioned above, but because the word 'bureaucratic' had become unpopular he adopted the alternative 'classical'. The scheme is therefore as follows:

### Styles of Leadership

| Traditional | Charismatic | Classical or bureaucratic | Human relations | Systemic or organic |
|---|---|---|---|---|
| Maintaining a tradition | Pursuing an intuition | Running a machine | Leading groups | Adapting a system |

Rudge himself argued for the systemic style but as we shall see there are occasions when one of the other styles is more appropriate. In any case the categories provide us with useful tools to analyse Christian leadership today. We shall be referring to them later but a preliminary description and assessment will be useful at this stage.

## Traditional leadership

This style has a great sense of history and values continuity with the past. In the church, such a leader sees his responsibility primarily in terms of handing on intact through the ministry of word and sacrament the historic riches of the faith. His authority rests in part on the fact that he is the fount of wisdom. The laity depend on the 'sacred elders' – bishops, archdeacons and priests – for guidance. This style was particularly suited to an age when there was little change taking place in society, but its weakness today is its failure to adapt to a fast changing world. Traditional leaders will faithfully expound the deposit of faith that has been entrusted to them and which must be handed on to each generation. In this they are following the advice of Paul to Timothy: 'And the things you have heard me say in the presence of many witnesses entrust to reliable men who will also be qualified to teach others' (2 Timothy 2:2); 'Guard what has been entrusted to your care' (1 Timothy 6:20). But traditional leaders are weak on relating the historic faith to the world of today. Their teaching programmes will major on theology and doctrine without tackling the issues that arise in their hearers' minds. One parishioner gave up attending his local Bible study group with these words: 'They spent hours debating the meaning of a single verse and would not allow me to raise the questions I wanted to ask.' Paul did not expect Timothy to pass on the truth woodenly and without application. Timothy had to 'correctly handle' (or divide) the word of truth (2 Timothy 2:15) and Paul's letters were a model of applying the unchanging Gospel to changing contemporary needs. The goal of Christian education for Paul was not simply that of information, but the formation of Christian character into the likeness of Christ. 'We proclaim him, admonishing and teaching everyone with all wisdom, so that we may present everyone perfect in Christ' (Colossians 1:28). The goal of the work of the ministry was that the 'body of Christ may be built up until we all reach unity in the faith and in the knowledge of the Son of God and become mature, attaining to the whole measure of the fulness of Christ' (Ephesians 4:12–13).

When he was a Pentecostal pastor in Argentina, Juan Carlos Ortiz used to combine central teaching with visits to the homes of members. If he undertook a series on 'the Christian family' he would call round to see how his teaching was being put into practice in family life. The traditional style needs to be balanced by the human relations and other styles, but it does have positive value. The opposite extreme is that of debating contemporary issues without relating the historic faith to them. We live in a day when unstructured house groups are in vogue, and one disillusioned member described his as 'a circle of people sharing their ignorance with unopened Bibles on their laps'.

In the past the traditional minister has been the unconscious model behind most ministerial training schemes. 'We are producing mini-theologians rather than maxi-pastors,' complained one missiologist. Ministers too easily became locked up in their studies rather than being let loose on the streets.

The programme of the traditional leader tends to focus on the unchanging round of rituals and ceremonials associated with the annual festivals. The agenda for the church committee will include the autumn bazaar, the nativity play and the Lent course, but there will be no strategies for mission. When leaders are under pressure as they frequently are it is tempting to take the easier course of following a recognised pattern rather than face the hard work of hammering out new strategies and programmes.

## Charismatic leadership

The charismatic leader is very different; his emphasis is a need to break with the past in order to go in new directions. The word 'charismatic' is used here in a sociological rather than in a spiritual sense and it describes a magnetic personality whose leadership is spontaneous and whose decisions arise from intuition, or a special sense of call, rather than being based on tradition or careful research. Those who follow his lead do so because they are attracted by his life, message or methods and not simply because they belong to the same organisation. Their support will, of course, lapse if and when the attraction wears off and so it cannot be taken for granted. Examples can be found both among the ministers of fashionable or well-attended churches and among ministers of struggling churches. This style may be particularly suited to para-church organisations or to voluntary agencies that are within the church but not part of its official structures; because they are not part of the official structure, support has to be attracted and cannot be coerced. Examples here include missionary societies and relief agencies. It is also valuable at national and international level within official church structures, especially when a spokesman is needed for the media. Journalists will pick up the comments of colourful, charismatic leaders, but are not usually excited by the resolutions of committees.

Charismatic leadership may be necessary when a church is moribund or when only one or two members are open to change. It may be unavoidable at an early stage of development when a church has few committed members. One such leader described new developments in his church as follows:

I took the bull by the horns and declared to all the people the nature of the church that we would be . . . I spelled out the whole scope of the vision. . . . It would have been so much easier to teach the truths and allow the people to decide for themselves. At this moment in time, however, it was necessary for the way ahead to be clearly charted and declared without debate. This was the way we were going. This was what God wanted. . . . There comes the time in the development of every church where the issues must be declared with unaffected authority from the word of God under the anointing of the Holy Spirit.[2]

The danger of charismatic leadership is that the members may become dependent on the leader and never mature, or that conflict may arise and be followed by a split. With charismatic leadership differences of opinion tend to be resolved by conflict rather than by discussion, or else strong personalities who disagree move elsewhere and only dependent personalities are left. It can often seem very 'successful', but success needs to be measured by the quality and maturity of other leaders' development, and not just by the quantity of members. Olan Hendrix has argued that the strong natural leader is of outstanding value in the early stages of an organisation, but can later become its own worst enemy.[3]

One answer is to have shared leadership which also includes elements of the classical and human relations style in order to provide for careful, consecutive planning and adequate pastoral care. To be led by a charismatic leader is fine when he is going in the right direction, but intuition needs to be checked. Tom Walker tells the story of a curate who led a hike up precipitous slopes and across impossible terrain. It was later discovered that although he was using a map, he had mistaken the county boundary for the footpath.[4] This kind of leader may have so many new ideas, plans and projects that his followers become bewildered and disorientated. As soon as they have adjusted to one direction they find he has moved off in another. Eventually disillusionment may set in. On the other hand life is not dull and many understandably prefer the excitement of charismatic to the predictability of traditional and classical leadership.

## Classical leadership

Bewilderment and disorientation are less likely with classical leadership. The appropriate diagram here is a pyramid one, with tight control from the top. The leader or minister is responsible for giving initiative and drive from the top, but also travels up and down the pyramid to check that each member is performing his appointed task. The virtue of this style is that it provides coherence, good organisation and careful planning. If the traditional style is typical of the Church of England the classical style is in general typical in the United States. There has been an exaggerated suspicion of transatlantic efficiency and organisation among British churches; we feel threatened by our American cousins and have often been slow to learn from them. Few British theological colleges give adequate training in management though it is becoming more common after ordination. The word 'administration', however, comes from the same root as 'ministry' and it is one of the gifts of the Spirit (1 Corinthians 12:28); a slipshod church is not honouring to God. Pastoral care of church members, for example, is more likely to be exercised effectively where there are careful records and a good system of organisation.

The danger of classical leadership, on the other hand, is that it can become remote and impersonal and organisational efficiency may become a barrier to close relationships. Efficiency and organisation need to be balanced by flexibility and sensitivity to people's needs. A new missionary fresh from a highly organised church in his home country announced to the congregation of a South American shanty town, 'I will be here to deal with pastoral problems on a Wednesday afternoon.' 'What happens if I have a problem on a Thursday?' was the reply. Classical leadership can work reasonably well in a congregation of sophisticated, literate and articulate businessmen who are used to reading reports on complex issues, but it can create impossible burdens for others. 'I never have time to read all the paper that comes out of the parish office,' complained one PCC member. The motives behind the paper were of the best. It was designed to promote widespread understanding and discussion before decisions were taken. It is difficult to organise democratic or synodical government in western society without a good deal of paper, but too often the average person cannot digest it and the debate is dominated by the minority who can. Few have the courage to admit at the meeting that they have not done their homework. The problem is especially acute in churches where the majority do not habitually read; they represent 60 per cent of the population in Britain. Classical leadership has too often imposed middle-class organisation in inner city areas, and western missionaries have placed similar burdens in third world countries. The unintended result may be middle-class or white domination. 'Our diocesan synod uses the papers and debating procedures of a western parliamentary system,' complained a black South African clergyman. 'Our people cannot cope with it and as a result the synod is dominated by the white minority.' There is a growing awareness that the style of debates in the General Synod of the Church of England may unintentionally inhibit some important sections of the population.

The classical leader may fail to develop human relationships and will improve means rather than accomplish ends. He starts by running a machine, but in the end the machine runs him. Ministers of this mould find their diaries so crowded with administrative tasks and committee meetings that there is little time left for ministry to people. A survey of urban ministers in the United States in 1956 revealed that the average minister spent 38 per cent of his time as an administrator and 12 per cent as an organiser. The biographies of bishops and archdeacons are replete with complaints that they find themselves becoming bureaucrats. It needs courage to hand over the chairmanship of committees to others.

## The human relations leader

This style of leadership concentrates on building a network of relationships, often through the creation of small groups. The groups usually meet in members' homes and their programme may include study, prayer, fellowship and service to the community, but the primary aim is to help members grow in their personal relationships. The strength of this approach is that it creates deep and caring fellowship and enables group members to develop to maturity. This is vitally important in an era where breakdown of family life and emotional damage is on the increase. If the charismatic leader is sometimes a dictator and the classical a bureaucrat, the human relations one is above all a counsellor. This style contains some elements of what has popularly been described as 'enabling leadership'. The leader refuses to undertake all the tasks of ministry himself, but draws out the gifts of others and equips them for ministry. At its best it mirrors Ephesians 4:11–12: 'It was he who gave some to be apostles, some to be prophets, some to be evangelists, and some to be pastors and teachers, to prepare God's people for works of service.'

Often associated with this style is an emphasis on 'non-directive counselling'. Many have encountered a hardpressed GP who seems to start writing out the prescription before they have had time to finish explaining the problem. His diagnosis and remedy may be right, but the patient finds it hard to believe that he has been listened to. Some Christian leaders use Bible verses as rapid umbrella prescriptions. The virtue of non-directive counselling on the other hand is that a person is helped to work through his problem himself with the help of a counsellor. This helps him to face the issues positively, to begin making constructive decisions about the future and to become less dependent therefore on the counsellor.

Unfortunately the success of non-directive counselling has led some into the mistake of attempting non-directive leadership. The latter is really a contradiction in terms; the 'enabling' leader who has no goals beyond the welfare of his groups and who gives no direction to them is really 'an enabling eunuch'. He is like a captain that is so busy ensuring that his crew are a happy, well-related team that he has no time to put out to sea.[5] The weakness of the human relations model is that on its own it can become inward looking and lack a proper concern and strategy for the church and for the community outside. At one stage a number of 'renewal churches' were falling into this trap. If the charismatic style provides direction and the classical style organisation without adequate pastoral concern, the human relations style tends to provide pastoral support without adequate direction or organisation.

## The systemic or organic model

A plant will adapt the direction of its development in order to grow towards the source of light, while a tree that is planted in rocky soil will spread its roots more widely to ensure stability. Just as a tree or plant adapts to its environment so the church under organic leadership adapts its policy, methods and organisation to the needs of a rapidly changing world. At the same time the plant, the tree and the church retain their basic nature, identity and roots. In terms of change it represents a style that comes midway between the charismatic one of abrupt and radical change and the traditional one of resisting or ignoring change. The traditional leader accepts the status quo, the charismatic rejects it and the organic leader promotes constant evolution and development. This can be illustrated by a parish that has an old-established community in one part with a traditional parish church at its centre. In another part is an industrial estate with new factories and offices and in another a new housing estate. The traditional leader will probably erect in the middle of the housing estate a new church building that mirrors the parish church in shape and furnishings. To exaggerate the illustration the charismatic might run a tent campaign, the classical plan a church office and the human relations leader a counselling centre. The systemic leader on the other hand may decide to hire a room at the estate primary school or at a pub in order to start worship and other activities. At a later stage he may erect a multi-purpose community centre that can also be used for worship. The direction of evolution and development is not, however, solely a matter of adapting to the environment; churches which simply do this end up by being carbon copies of other community organisations. The organic leader is also concerned to develop in the direction set by the church's own goals and objectives. One such goal might be the deepening of fellowship and so a number of meetings will be held in members' homes; another will be social concern and there might develop a number of cells or action groups in the industrial estate concerned with specific social issues.

The word 'systemic' describes a system which is made up of constituent parts but which is greater than the sum of those parts. In this respect it comes between the classical style of a single pyramid structure and the human relations style of unrelated groups. The systemic organisation provides a framework, link or system between groups to give them a unifying purpose. The different models are illustrated in the diagrams overleaf.

The traditional model is like a bottle, where the leaders can become the bottleneck in decision-making and action, but also like a Gothic church where the 'sacred elders' dispense grace from the sanctuary. The charismatic model typifies direction and change and so is in the shape of an arrow. One of the limitations of the systemic model is that it does not suggest movement and change, but it serves to demonstrate the difference from the unrelated groups of

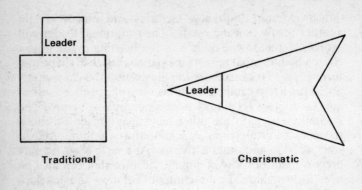

**Traditional**                                  **Charismatic**

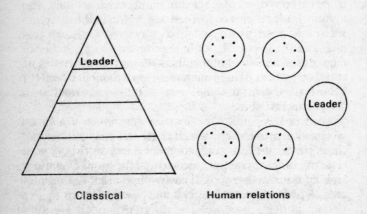

**Classical**                         **Human relations**

the human relations model. Leadership will not be just from the 'top' or from the 'centre', as in the traditional, classical and charismatic styles, but will be exercised at different points in the system according to need. The outer circles in the diagram may represent leaders of youth work, evangelism and worship. Decisions affecting these areas of church life will primarily be taken in the appropriate circle though with reference to and from the circle of leaders in

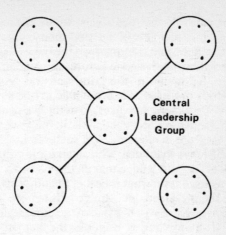

Central
Leadership
Group

Systemic

the centre, and this circle will include representatives from the outer circles. This is illustrated more fully in Chapter 7. The task of the systemic leader is not to provide all the direction and drive as in the classical model, nor is it to forget the need for direction and drive as in the human relations one. His functions include the prophetic ones of interpreting the changes taking place in the world and in the church, of clarifying purpose and direction and of monitoring and correcting goals. This will lead to a continuing adjustment and redefinition of individual tasks.

## The right style

As we have seen, the first four styles all contain ingredients that are essential to Christian leadership. The traditional gives continuity with the past, the charismatic direction, the classical organisation and the human relations pastoral concern. These positive elements all find support in scripture. Peter Rudge links the different metaphors used for the church with the various styles; the traditional leader emphasises the 'people of God' and their continuity with the past, the charismatic emphasises the 'new creation' and the break with what has gone before, the human relations leader the 'fellowship in the faith' and the systemic the organic 'Body of Christ'. He is not able to find a metaphor in the New Testament, however, to fit the classical theory.[6] All these emphases are valid, but if they are taken in isolation they are inadequate. We shall see in Chapter 11 how the different styles deal with change and conflict.

We can agree with Rudge that on the whole the systemic style seems to contain what is best in the other styles and is therefore the preferred one. Rudge fails to note, however, that there are occasions when one of the other styles is more suitable. If counselling is required the human relations approach may be best. If a fire breaks out in the organ loft then a charismatic call to action is needed, not non-directive discussion. If an organisation has bad administration it may need to call in a leader of the classical style. The ideal is a shared leadership as described in Chapter 5 which includes leaders with differing gifts and styles working as a team. It is all too easy to assume that the style we know best, the one we have used in the past or the one that most suits our personality, is the best or preferred one. It will depend not only on our gifts, but also on the need of the hour and the stage of development in an organisation. The most essential task for the Christian leader is to understand the differences between the styles, to evaluate their advantages and disadvantages and to decide which is appropriate for each occasion. The following chapters are designed to help in this evaluation.

# 2 CHIEFTAIN, PATRON, GURU OR EXECUTIVE?

Leadership around the world.

The influence of local culture on styles of leadership.

Are styles of leadership universal or adapted to local needs?

What can we learn from other countries?

We live in a shrinking world. An increasing number of us travel to other countries, whether as holidaymakers, business executives or missionaries. If we follow the tourist routes we find that life can be very similar, but if we go elsewhere, especially in the third world, we find striking variety. If we become involved with the local church overseas we discover that patterns of church life and leadership have been shaped by local culture and can be very different from our own. The more observant visitor then begins to ask questions – 'If church life overseas is shaped by local culture then how far is my local church life in Britain shaped by British culture and not simply based on unchanging universal principles?' There are lessons to be learnt from churches in other countries and very often we cannot stand back from our own culture until we have experienced another one either at first or second hand. We cannot do justice in a single chapter to the variety of leadership styles throughout the world. It is sufficient to select a few in order to show how often leadership in the church mirrors that in society.

## Examples in Asia and Africa

Vinay Samuel and Chris Sugden describe Asian society in general as being feudal in structure:

> Power rests not in social organisation but in individuals, to whom power has been handed over because they are sons of parents who have demonstrated the ability to use power for the benefit of those they rule. The feudal pattern survives because it creates dependency in the powerless. . . . The Asian tradition is one of deference to others who are older, wiser and appointed by the destiny of birth allowing them to determine the course of common people's lives. . . . Sadly churches are often affected by the feudalistic pattern of leadership so powerful in surrounding society.[1]

In Japan there is strong dynamic leadership both in society and in the church; Confucianism traditionally accords great respect to the 'teacher' and the Christian pastor can unconsciously or consciously take on this role.

In India it may be the spirituality of a person that gives him or her authority. The most famous example is Mother Teresa; her shining personality, deep devotion and sacrificial work has attracted thousands. This appeals far more than the slick evangelist from the West, armed with every modern method of communication.

Charismatic leadership is common in African society, especially in tribal areas. On one occasion an African bishop invited us to travel with him as he visited a number of rural churches. In the course of a few hours and an incalculable number of miles he married several and confirmed hundreds. On each occasion he was welcomed as if he were a tribal chief. In himself he was a humble and a gracious man, but his style of leadership was modelled partly on the chieftain and partly on the style exported by missionaries of an earlier generation.

## Pentecostals in Chile – leaders who are 'of the people'

In Britain we find the church flourishing in a number of suburban districts but in few inner city or Urban Priority Areas. Yet in Chile the church is growing in Urban Priority Areas at a rate of 10 per cent per annum. One Pentecostal 'cathedral' near the centre of the capital has a membership list of 80,000. The congregation are drawn from all over the city and are asked to attend only once a month on a rota basis, while on other Sundays they worship in their own locality.

What is the secret of this remarkable growth? The urban scene in Chile is in many respects different from ours in Britain, but there are some principles that can be transferred. The style of leadership in Pentecostal churches meets people at their point of need. Peasants who flock into the shanty towns surrounding the cities are wrenched by economic forces from the protective 'family' of the large rural estate. The population may have grown too large or the estate may have been mechanised, or both. The city will have been presented through commercial radio as the place where 'the good things of life' can be found. They come looking for work, schools and medical help, but are also seeking friendship and security.

They need a new father figure and find it in their pastor. The Pentecostal leader is charismatic in every sense and his style is a mixture of the Indian chief, the landowning 'patron' and the military 'caudillo' or dictator. Leadership in Pentecostal churches meets people at their point of need and mirrors leadership in society; it is therefore effective. However, the pastor is not an isolated dictator; he will often have no more than primary education and will come from an artisan background. His people will see him as 'one of us'. He will also encourage others to be trained for leadership at every level. The new convert is soon witnessing in open-air evangelism, may then be asked to lead a street corner service, and may progress through Sunday school leadership to becoming an assistant pastor. The pathway to leadership is not an academic one; preparation is on the streets rather than in the study and often a man cannot become a pastor until he has planted a new church. By this criterion few British ministers of mainline churches would be in leadership positions today. A suspicion of academic study has its dangers but the Pentecostal method means that the pathway to leadership is open to all. Western leadership is usually more democratic, but it is the kind of democracy where doors in society and the church are usually open only to the educated and articulate. Our road to leadership is restricted to a professional elite and this is why we fail in Urban Priority Areas. The lesson of shared leadership will be dealt with in Chapter 5 and the implications for leadership training in Chapter 12; the 'servant' principle, being 'one of the people', is expounded in Chapter 9.

## Base communities in Brazil – leadership from within

Base or basic communities are a relatively recent phenomenon. They are best known as a feature of Roman Catholic church life in Latin America, but they have been established in other countries and in other denominations. It is estimated that there may be as many as 100,000 in Brazil alone. In contrast to the large 'celebration' of the Pentecostal the base communities are a kind of house church with a membership of between twenty-five and fifty. This makes them larger than the traditional house group, but smaller than a congregation and it can therefore be argued that this optimum size is small enough to create deep fellowship, but big enough to provide a rich range of personalities and gifts. The smaller house group can at times be too restrictive. They often meet in a house or in some other local building, but not normally in a church. Unlike the house church movement the base communities see themselves as part of the main denomination, normally the Church of Rome. They meet not only to build up their spiritual life, but also to relate the Christian faith to local social and political issues. Their discussion will deal with drains as well as doctrine, with the need for a water supply as well as with spirituality, and this discussion will often lead to lobbying, action and even protest. The base communities present a fascinating model of alternative leadership. The leader will be local, one of the people, thrown up from within and below rather than imposed from outside and above. As such he is unlikely to impose styles of worship, language and learning that are foreign. His agenda will be seen to be relevant. This approach allows ordinary people to have a share in shaping their future, in strict contrast to their position in society and at work.

Again there are lessons here for leadership in Britain, especially in Urban Priority Areas. Like the Pentecostal pastor the base community leader is one of the people, but unlike the Pentecostal he is a layman. The parish priest is not himself the leader, but acts as a consultant who is brought in as required. We shall see some British models of consultant leadership alongside managerial leadership in Chapter 7. The base community leader's agenda, perhaps because he is not a professional, deals with socio-political and not just with spiritual or ecclesiastical issues; this theme will be taken up in Chapter 8. Again one of the secrets of growth in numbers and of a leadership explosion is a willingness to share leadership and to share with those who would normally be passed over in a western democracy.

## Individualistic or group approaches – which are appropriate?

Western society is largely fragmented and individualistic, but in tribal societies there is often a preference for a group approach and a group response. In 'people's movements' a whole tribe or part of a tribe is baptised at the same time, whereas an individual converted or baptised on his own would become a social outcast. No doubt a similar situation existed with household baptisms in the New Testament; when Lydia was baptised her whole household was baptised at the same time (Acts 16:15) and the same was true of the Philippian jailer. Parallels can be found in some forms of youth work in Britain today. It may be unwise to press an individual member of a gang into making a decision to become a committed Christian until a majority of the gang are ready to do the same, otherwise the individual will become isolated and a social outcast and will find it difficult to go on as a Christian. We certainly found this in work with heroin addicts in West London.

The question of whether to use an individualistic or group approach is relevant in discussing appropriate forms of leadership. Many in Urban Priority Areas in the West will find group leadership an easier route to gaining sufficient confidence. Bishop David Sheppard describes how George Burton of the Mayflower Centre in East London would never ask an individual to take a lead, but would always ask two or three, or even seven or eight. 'The group gave confidence to one another, made it enjoyable and kept the momentum going when someone had a "down" patch.'[2] We shall see from Chapter 5 that shared leadership was common in New Testament times and one of the reasons behind the church's ineffectiveness in difficult areas in Britain is our failure to follow this pattern.

In any form of shared or group leadership an appropriate method has to be found for reaching decisions. Again cultural factors are important. Western decision-making processes require an ability to read and articulate. In many tribal societies, however, a consensus will be reached and the leader will identify and express that consensus without taking a vote. This may take longer but it has the merit that it avoids a polarisation forcing one side to feel it has lost. In some areas in the West the local culture will require leadership through group consensus rather than by a confrontational debate where the articulate dominate. What is meant by 'consensus'? It can be taken as equivalent to unanimity implying that the group will not move forward until unanimity is reached. It can, however, represent an approach that comes midway between unanimity and the rule of the majority vote. 'Consensus' can mean that the minority consent to the way forward even if it is not the way they would have chosen, while on the other hand the majority refuse to go forward unless the minority consent.[3]

## Mega-church Leadership in the United States

The mega-churches in the United States have huge congregations, a large staff and a complex of buildings providing not only meeting rooms, but also counselling rooms, canteens, squash courts and a whole range of other facilities. I remember preaching in one church which had a staff of forty; after the sermon we took a lift to the fifth floor for group discussion.

The style of leadership found in many mega-churches in the United States is very different from that found in the base communities. The model taken from the business world is that of an efficient organiser, company executive or president. The pastor is removed from everyday affairs in order to run the organisation. Peter Wagner quotes with approval the mega-church pastor who refused to visit his members in their homes or in hospital or to do any one-to-one counselling.[4] There is a valid point here. The minister may be so immersed in the detail of daily ministry that he never has time to think and pray through goals and objectives; those who spend their time tinkering with nuts and

bolts cannot adequately supervise a large factory. Yet a
minister who is too removed from the grassroots may be
unable to appreciate the needs of the flock. Unlike the base
community leader he may be slow to appreciate the importance of relating faith to social and political issues. Is there a
link between the remoteness of this mega-church leadership and the growth of a right-wing 'moral majority'? Peter
Wagner may, of course, be overstating his case in order to
make a point, but it is not easy to see how the model he
portrays fits in with the ideal of *servant* leadership as
described in Chapter 9.

## Britain – a variety of cultures

If styles of leadership have been shaped by cultural factors
in other countries we should not be surprised to find that
this is so in Britain. Not that we have a monochrome,
unchanging culture; our sociological and ethnic mix provides rich variety and this mix may vary from one decade to
another. Within the variety, however, it is possible to
discern some general trends. In the 1940s there was a
readiness to accept strong leadership, whether from a
politician like Winston Churchill or from a general like
Montgomery. They were heroes to be followed and
admired without too much questioning, and if they had
faults those faults were not normally exposed by the media.
Similarly strong leadership was the order of the day in the
church.

In the 1940s and the 1950s the laity were there to help the
clergy, not to question them. Even in the 1960s it was
common for a minister to feel he ought to resign if his
church council rejected one of his major proposals. Partnership between laity and clergy was one of horse and rider.
After the 1940s higher education became more widely
available and it became normal to question every assumption, institution and leader. Nothing was to be taken for
granted. We entered a period when many were diffident at

taking on leadership. In 1976 Montgomery complained 'because of muddled thinking about equality many sections of Western democratic society are suspicious of the whole idea of the necessity for leadership and of the need for any special training'.[5] In churches open to change there was an emphasis on 'every member ministry' and on 'Body ministry' with every member of the church, the Body of Christ, having a special gift and a differing ministry. However, this change lacked a complementary stress on the need for good leadership. 'We have so emphasised the priesthood of all believers', complained one minister in the Midlands, 'that we have forgotten the need for leadership.' Without leadership 'every member ministry' can become inward looking and lack the mission goals that compel the body of believers to act and witness in the world.

More recently the pendulum has swung again. Society now looks for strong, dynamic leadership. A powerful personality at 10 Downing Street is someone to be respected, whatever we may feel about the government's policies. This tendency is mirrored in the new house church movement which provides a strong, authoritarian leadership. Members are expected to be discipled by submitting to the authority of those appointed over them as elders and shepherds. In some cases this can be healthy; in others it is taken to extremes with minute guidance being given over every aspect of the disciple's life, whether work, marriage or family. Some aspects of this desire for strong leadership give cause for concern. At its worst it represents a desire to shelve responsibility and to let others take the blame for mistakes.

Within these general trends there are a variety of cultural differences. In the stockbroker belt there will be those used to leadership roles even if their skills are not always harnessed by the church. In the inner city will be some who have been socialised into dependency, and as a result ministers traditionally complain 'there is no leadership potential in this area'. In fact there is. There will be some who are used to leadership in trade union and other spheres

but have been put off the local church either because it only
attracts inadequate or dependent people or because its
style of operation is middle-class.

It is essential to compare styles of leadership in other
cultures in order to evaluate our own. Leadership is likely
to be more effective when it meets people's expectations
and needs, either because it mirrors leadership in society or
because it meets a need which is not being fulfilled in
society. Sometimes, of course, expectations and needs
are diametrically opposed. In the 1970s a church in East
London tried the courageous experiment of ordaining four
dockers in order to demonstrate the validity and importance of establishing a local, artisan, shared leadership. The
experiment was largely a failure because the dockers did
not fulfil the traditional expectations of what a minister was
like. It is greatly to be hoped that this kind of experiment
can be repeated in a more acceptable way, but traditional
expectations cannot be ignored as we consider the method
and pace of change.

## Our attitude to culture

The argument so far is that we ought to be ready to adapt
our styles of leadership to suit the culture of the country or
area concerned and the needs and expectations of the
people. However, there are principles of leadership to be
found in scripture that are of universal validity – in all
places and at all times – and these principles must be
allowed to judge and modify all cultures. One example will
suffice at this point. When Jesus became man he became a
particular man in a specific culture at a special point in
history. In general he was ready to identify with Jewish
culture, but at certain points he was ready to challenge it in
order to show a better way. His relationship to the twelve
was very similar to that of a rabbi to his followers. However, he forbad the use of titles such as 'teacher' or 'father'.
Perhaps the greatest contrast comes in Mark 10, where

James and John had been asking for a privileged seat in heaven; they wanted to sit on either side of Jesus. Jesus calls the other ten to him and says, 'You know that those who are regarded as rulers of the Gentiles lord it over them, and their high officials exercise authority over them. Not so with you. Instead, whoever wants to become great among you must be your servant, and whoever wants to be first must be slave of all. For even the Son of Man did not come to be served, but to serve, and to give his life as a ransom for many' (vv 42–5). Jesus turns his back on the authoritarian style of leadership found in the society of his day and instead advocates a servant style. An autocratic style of leadership, whether traditional, charismatic or classical, whether in a Latin American Pentecostal or a North American Baptist, cannot therefore be justified whatever the patterns of society or the expectations of people.

The early church refused to impose Jewish culture on Gentile converts (see p. 160) and we must refuse to impose our culture on other areas, whether from suburban Surrey to inner city Brixton or from industrial Britain to rural Africa. At the same time there are universal principles of leadership by which all cultures must be judged; we shall see these in the next chapter.

# 3 PROPHET, PRIEST, KING, ELDER

## Leadership in Bible times

What were the types of leadership in Old Testament times?

How were these altered in the New Testament?

Is there a Bible blueprint for leadership and ministry?

God chooses unlikely leaders. The pages of the Old Testament give fascinating biographies of a wide variety of people called into leadership positions. Who would have expected a cunning schemer like Jacob or a bumptious boaster like Joseph to be used by God? We see God's patience with Moses first as he kills an Egyptian in protest against oppression and then as he is too unsure of himself to be God's spokesman after forty years' domestication in the desert (Genesis 25–41; Exodus 2–4). God demonstrates again and again that he can shape leaders as a potter shapes clay. There are countless leadership lessons to be learnt from the pages of the Bible,[1] yet our purpose in this chapter is to focus on whether there are Bible blueprints for leadership structures and styles rather than on the personalities of particular leaders. To do this we shall have to distinguish between patterns which are descriptive and those which are prescriptive; i.e. those that simply describe the forms of leadership at a particular place or in a particular period and

those which prescribe a pattern to be followed at all times
and in all places. We shall see that in practice the forms of
leadership in Bible times often reflected the culture of the
day and the forms in society around. Michael Green,
writing about ministry in the New Testament period, has
said:

> We should be foolish to look for a precise blueprint for
> 'the ministry' in the pages of the New Testament. For
> one thing those pages tell a story of staggering diver-
> sity. Congregationalists, Presbyterians, Episcopalians,
> Brethren and Roman Catholics can all point to some
> element in ministry in the New Testament as justifica-
> tion. Most of the advances derive from the needs of the
> situation rather than from any preconceived normative
> plan.[2]

Yet while there may not be a *precise* blueprint for forms of
ministry and leadership we shall see that there is certainly a
general blueprint for principles of leadership.

## Leadership in the Old Testament

The main forms to be found in the Old Testament are those
of prophet, priest and king. In the earlier periods some of
these roles were combined. Samuel had both a prophetic
and a judicial role and both David and Solomon seem to
have exercised some priestly functions (2 Samuel 6:13ff;
1 Kings 8:5). The early nomadic tribes were led by the
patriarchs, beginning with Abraham. Their leadership
could fairly be described as paternalistic and it has some
parallels with the traditional style described in Chapter 1.
From the Exodus to the conquest of Palestine the people of
Israel were led by Moses and Joshua, non-hereditary rulers
of a charismatic kind. Yet even a charismatic leader like
Moses learnt to share his leadership with others. There is an
interesting episode recorded in the book of Numbers where

he complains, 'I cannot carry all these people by myself; the burden is too heavy for me.' The Lord replies, 'Bring me seventy of Israel's elders who are known to you as leaders and officials among the people. . . . I will take of the Spirit that is on you and put the Spirit on them. They will help you carry the burden of the people' (Numbers 11:14, 16, 17). If Abraham was a traditional leader and Moses a charismatic we could say that the Old Testament priesthood was nearest to the classical style.

## Priests and prophets

The patriarchs seem to have exercised the priestly functions of prayer, blessing, sacrifice and teaching, and Moses apparently combined the roles of prophet and priest, though specific priestly functions were delegated to his brother Aaron. The priesthood became established through Aaron's successors and the priest had the responsibility of sacrifice, of teaching the law and of providing specific guidance on request.[3] The prophet on the other hand had the responsibility both of proclamation and prediction, of forthtelling and foretelling. His office was not hereditary like the priest's, but depended on a special call to deliver God's word to the nation and to individuals within it. The prophets reminded the nation of its call to the social and moral righteousness of the covenant, while the king had the responsibility of establishing that righteousness (Isaiah 11:1–5). Although the prophets were sometimes associated with the royal court they were primarily independent both of the ecclesiastical and the civil establishment. The institutions of prophet and priest were to be found in surrounding nations, but Israel's prophets differed from their contemporaries in that they were independent from the official establishment, their message was not ephemeral or commonplace and they were concerned with national and international morality and justice; their God was Lord of all the nations. Unfortunately all three institutions – prophet, priest and king – went through periods of corruption. Jeremiah records: 'Both prophet and priest are godless' (Jeremiah 23:11).

One of the most significant episodes for our purposes was the debate between Samuel and the elders over the question of appointing a king.

## The debate over kingship

Although prophets, priests and kings could be found in other nations Israel had been different from other nations in being a theocracy – a nation under the direct control of God. The period of the Judges had shown, however, that even a theocracy needs an established and recognised leader, who acts as God's representative. The repeated refrain is, 'In those days Israel had no king; everyone did as he saw fit' (Judges 21:25). It is the elders who voice the desire for a king: 'Appoint a king to lead us, such as all the other nations have' (1 Samuel 8:5). They call for a form of leadership that is patterned on society around. Samuel declares that this request represents a rejection of the Lord as king (v 7), but the Lord later reveals Saul as his choice for the new king (9:16). At first reading this seems a contradiction and some Old Testament scholars have argued that there are two different strands in the records, one in favour of kingship and one against. Whether or not this is so we can here trace the working out of God's purposes in history whereby he takes into account his people's weakness and failure and shapes his plans accordingly. In theory it would have been possible to have had a theocratic kingship where the king depended on divine guidance as much as Samuel and the other prophets did. Was the difference that kingship was considered to be hereditary and therefore the throne would be handed on automatically without God's guidance being sought, however unsuitable the successor? On the other hand the priesthood was hereditary. What is perhaps being condemned here is not kingship as such but a rejection of theocracy; it is the motives and implication of the request, not the request itself that is at fault.

## Leaders are subject to God's law

Even though the Lord allows Israel to have a form of leadership similar to other nations the way that leadership is exercised is to be different. God's covenant was direct with the people, not mediated by the king, and so Israel had no 'divine right' of kings. The king, like his subjects, is to be subservient to the law of God, and prophets are raised up to remind him of this fact. This can be illustrated from the story of Naboth's vineyard, recorded in 1 Kings 21. Queen Jezebel comes from another culture and can therefore see no problem in Ahab seizing the vineyard if he wants it. Kings do that sort of thing in other nations. But Elijah is sent to pronounce divine judgment on Ahab for flouting the law of God. Similarly Nathan rebukes King David for his adultery with Bathsheba and his murder of her husband (2 Samuel 12). Prophets were also given the authority on occasion to anoint new kings (1 Kings 19:16 and 1 Samuel 16); this was a risky business if the reigning king was still on the throne.

## Christ fulfils Old Testament forms of leadership

As all three forms became corrupt the prophets began to look for an ideal leader, the Messiah, who would embody the three roles of prophet, priest and king. ' "Woe to the shepherds who are destroying and scattering the sheep of my pasture!" declares the Lord. . . . "Both prophet and priest are godless. . . . The days are coming when I will raise up to David a righteous Branch, a King who will reign wisely and do what is just and right in the land" ' (Jeremiah 23:1, 11 and 5). Christ is therefore the ideal leader and the model for styles of leadership. Christian ministry and leadership are exercised in, through and for him, or rather Christ exercises his ministry in and through the Christian leader fulfilling the prophetic task of proclamation, the priestly role of reconciliation and the supervision or oversight embodied in kingship.

## Is leadership necessary in the church?

One very significant difference between the Old Testament and the New is that *every* Christian receives the gift and gifts of the Holy Spirit in order to share in Christ's ministry of prophet, priest and king. The apostle John wrote to the seven churches of Asia in these words: 'To him who loves us and has freed us from our sins by his blood, and has made us to be a kingdom and priests' (Revelation 1:5–6). The New Testament teaches the priesthood of all believers but it is not so frequently remembered that it also teaches the kingship of all believers. Every Christian has a priestly responsibility of representing God to man and man to God, but he also has the kingly privilege of sharing the throne and rule of Christ – 'God raised us up with Christ and seated us with him in the heavenly realms' (Ephesians 2:6). In one sense Christ is our ruler and in another sense every Christian is a ruler; this means that no form of autocratic leadership can be justified in the church. Does it mean that human leadership within the church is unnecessary? In recent years there has been an increasing emphasis on 'Body ministry' stressing that every Christian is a member of the body of Christ and has one or more gifts for ministry (1 Corinthians 12:11–12). We used to say that a person training for ordination was 'going into the church' but this phrase was dropped in recognition of the fact that every Christian is a member of the church. Later we used the phrase 'going into the ministry' but this obscured the fact that every Christian is 'in the ministry'. The emphasis on 'Body ministry' has been important and good, but it has

sometimes obscured the need for leadership within the
body of Christ, with disastrous results. Indeed one of Paul's
primary purposes in writing his first letter to the church at
Corinth was to emphasise the need for recognised leadership to have proper oversight of the exercise of spiritual
gifts. We shall see below that leaders were established in
the early church but that New Testament leadership was
within and with the people of God rather than outside and
over them. Ministers are to be regarded, for example, as
part of the laity or people (*laos*) of God and not separate
from them.

## Leadership in the early church

The apostles take the lead in the early chapters of Acts and
then as the pressure increases they delegate the more
administrative tasks to seven others. 'It would not be right
for us to neglect the ministry of the word of God in order to
wait on tables . . . choose seven men from among you . . .
we will turn this responsibility over to them' (Acts 6:2–3).
Are we right to give the title 'deacon' to these seven? They
are often quoted as the prototype of modern deacons. The
word 'deacon' is not used as such and while the word for
'wait' in 'waiting on tables' is 'diakoneo' it is also the case
that the word 'ministry' in the apostles' 'ministry of the
word' is 'diakonia'. In any case we soon find two of the
seven – Stephen and Philip – busily engaged in preaching,
evangelism and signs and wonders (Acts 6:8–15 and 8:4–8).

It is clear that there was a good deal more variety than is
often the case today. The apostle Paul travelled round the
Eastern Mediterranean, founding churches. He made provision for leadership in those churches by appointing elders
(Acts 14:23), and in the case of Crete he commissioned
Titus to appoint elders on his behalf – 'The reason I left you
in Crete was that you . . . might appoint elders in every
town' (Titus 1:5). Some maintain that this pattern of elders
was universal and therefore mandatory. There is some

debate, however, on whether elders were ever appointed in Corinth. They are not mentioned in the list in 1 Corinthians 12:28, though helpers and administrators are. Marjorie Warkentin claims that there were different patterns in Corinth and Ephesus.[4] However, it could be argued that 1 Corinthians 12:28 gives a list of gifts rather than offices and certainly the Letter of Clement, written towards the end of the first century, mentions elders at Corinth. Even if they were not there at the beginning the state of the church would have called for some such appointment.

Elders are not included in the list of offices in Ephesians 4:11, but the church at Ephesus clearly had them. In Acts 20:17 Paul is recorded as summoning 'the elders of the church' to meet him at Miletus. Are they to be identified with the apostles, prophets, pastors and teachers of Ephesians 4:11 or just with the pastors and teachers, or what? We shall discuss this below (pp. 50–53).

The word 'bishop' appears in the New Testament in several places. Paul designates his letter to the Philippians, 'To all the saints . . . with the bishops and deacons' (1:1 RSV). Elders are not mentioned as such and Bishop Lightfoot has shown that the two words 'bishop' and 'elder' are virtually interchangeable.[5] During the second century, however, the office of bishop separated from that of elder or presbyter. The bishop became in effect the chairman of the group of elders or the presiding elder. There is certainly value in having a system of leadership that is wider than the local church. It is interesting that the modern house church movement has developed a system of 'apostles' who have an oversight rather like a bishop. Methodists, too, have their superintendents. This creates partnership between churches and ensures that the stronger help the weak.

## Is there a New Testament blueprint?

Undoubtedly Michael Green is right in saying there is no *precise* blueprint for the forms of ministry (p. 41); most

denominations can find a basis for the form of leadership
they use today. Even if we could prove that the appointment of elders was universal in practice this does not
necessarily prove that the pattern is normative for all times
and all places. It could simply be an illustration of the
practice of adopting styles of leadership known in society at
large. Elders were the backbone of most communities in
the ancient world and they were to be found in Old
Testament Israel. We have seen how Moses delegated
some of his authority to elders and that it was the elders of
Israel who petitioned Samuel for a king (pp. 42–3). In New
Testament times the leaders of the Jewish synagogues were
known as elders and it seems as if the early church adopted
this title, perhaps to suggest continuity. Nor was the synagogue the only model. The basic unit of society was the
household and this unit could include not only the extended
family but also slaves, freedmen, hired workers, tenants
and partners. We read of the church which met in the house
of Prisca and Aquila, for example (Romans 16:5). Often
the head of the household became the leader of the church,
as seems to have been the case with Lydia (Acts 16). It
seems that the church was happy to borrow forms of
leadership and patterns of organisation from society at
large.

In distinguishing descriptive from prescriptive we have to
ask which patterns and models are simply reflecting the
culture of the day and which are intended to be the norm for
all places and all times. However, there is a very important
position midway between these two alternatives and that is
to suggest that there are universal theological principles
which affect both the choice of models and the way they are
exercised. The universal principle of love will, for example,
make it very difficult to justify the choice of tyranny as a
model however much it may be the norm in society. We
have already seen that Christ's servant principle will rule
out an autocratic style. Our task therefore is to fashion
forms of leadership that are consonant as far as possible
with the culture of the day but are also consonant with those

universal Christian principles by which culture is to be modified and purified. Even if we agree that there is no *precise* or detailed blueprint there are a number of principles that go towards a general blueprint for leadership. Seven of these are given a preliminary description below and most will be discussed more fully in subsequent chapters.

> *Seven Principles of Leadership*
> 1. Leadership is to be shared
> 2. Leadership is for equipping others
> 3. Leadership is varied
> 4. Leadership is flexible
> 5. Leadership is to be both settled and mobile
> 6. Leaders are to be servants
> 7. Leaders include both men and women

## 1. Leadership is to be shared

In the New Testament the words 'elder' or 'bishop' are nearly always to be found in the plural; this is significant and no accident. In Philippians 1:1 Paul writes, 'To all the saints . . . with the bishops and deacons' (RSV). There is no hint of the omnicompetent one-man-band style of ministry; different members of the body have different gifts and tasks and even the leadership gifts are varied. God has therefore so arranged his church that we have to be dependent on one another and need the support and help of a leadership group. The practical outworking of this principle is discussed in Chapter 5.

## 2. Leadership is for equipping others

If every Christian is 'in the ministry' (p. 45) then the task of the Christian leader is to 'equip the saints for the work of ministry' (Ephesians 4:12 RSV), not to do all the work of ministry on behalf of the saints. The word translated 'equip' is a rich one used in different places with a variety of meanings; it can be used of repairing what is broken, restoring what is lost, and supplying what is defective. This equipping, according to Hebrews 13:20, is part of the ministry of God himself, our chief leader or shepherd.

A useful distinction can be made between gift, office and function, provided that the word 'office' is seen in terms of activity rather than status. Several Christians in a local church will have the special gift of teaching, but not all will be appointed to leadership or to the office of 'teacher'. On the other hand most Christians will have to function as teachers from time to time, whether as a parent instructing a child, or as a mature Christian teaching a new convert. The leader who has the office of teacher has a responsibility to equip the saints to become effective in their teaching of others. Timothy is instructed to find faithful men 'who will be able to teach others also' (2 Timothy 2:2 RSV).

## 3. Leadership is varied

Not only do church members vary in their gifts, but so do leaders. 1 Corinthians 12 describes the varied gifts given to members of the church so that they become dependent on one another: 'The eye cannot say to the hand, "I don't need you!"' (v 21); the teacher cannot say to the administrator, 'I don't need you!' Variety is needed so that the church as a whole can have the full range of gifts and ministries both for the benefit of members and for effective service to the world at large. Michael Harper has drawn on Ephesians 4:11 to give an interesting scheme of leadership ministry. He claims that the work of apostles, prophets, evangelists, pastors and teachers represent five functions of the church –

Let my people go – the apostolic function of the church
Let my people hear – the prophetic function of the church
Let my people care – the pastoral function of the church

Let my people know – the teaching function of the
  church
Let my people grow – the evangelistic function of the
  church[6]

This scheme has value in illustrating the variety of leadership functions, but there are questions that need to be
faced. The first is whether any of the lists of leadership and
ministry functions in the New Testament are meant to be
exhaustive. Certainly the list of gifts in 1 Corinthians 12 is
different at some points from the list in Romans 8 and the
list of leadership appointments in Ephesians 4:11 is different from that in 1 Corinthians 12:27–30, though the latter
may be a mixture of leadership and other ministries. It
seems that the functions were not always clearly demar-
cated. Timothy seems to have been primarily a pastor and
teacher, but he is also asked to 'do the work of an evangelist' (2 Timothy 4:5). In the pastoral epistles the general
emphasis is on elders who teach as well as exercise pastoral
care, but it seems that not all did – 'The elders who direct
the affairs of the church well are worthy of double honour,
especially those whose work is preaching and teaching' (1
Timothy 5:17). James 5:14 shows the elders engaged in
prayer for healing. Because the distinctions are not water-
tight Eddie Gibbs portrays the leadership ministries of
Ephesians 4:11 as a series of overlapping circles (see the
diagram overleaf).[7] But even this scheme is too 'organised'
to represent the New Testament pattern. It is likely that in
Ephesians 4:11 Paul is describing the universal church and
not just the local church; he therefore includes both local
and itinerant ministries.

It is also likely that there was greater variety and flexibility in the earlier New Testament period and that leadership
roles became settled as time went on, though this does
not mean that even the later period is normative. Nor is it
clear that all those described in this verse were *necessarily*
leaders. Not all ministry is leadership ministry; it is clear
that those with gifts of evangelism or teaching are to train

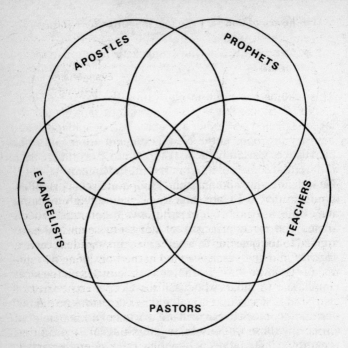

others to evangelise and teach and to that extent they are to 'give a lead', but this does not make them part of the team that had general oversight of the church. Some evangelists will train others 'on the job' while some will set up and co-ordinate a programme for others to fulfil. A medical example of the former is a consultant with his team of students and an example of the latter is a hospital administrator. It may mean that if we are to draw circles we can only draw two, and they completely overlap!

What we can clearly argue is that every Christian has a gift or gifts and is called to exercise ministry. Some are called to leadership and they, too, will have a variety of gifts. There will be several such leaders in each local church. Leadership is varied and flexible and therefore has to be a team exercise.

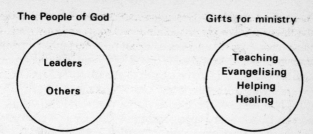

**4. Leadership is flexible**

We have seen how Stephen and Philip were set apart for an administrative task, but soon found themselves preaching and evangelising. Different patterns were followed as need arose. The same principle of flexibility seems to have applied to the question of whether leaders should receive a salary. On many occasions Paul earned his living by tent-making (Acts 20:33–5) so as not to be a burden on the local church and to demonstrate that the Gospel comes free of charge (2 Corinthians 11:7). On other occasions he did not hesitate to receive money and to issue a challenge to Christian giving (2 Corinthians 8 and 9). It is good that greater flexibility is being experienced in churches today, including the question of salary payments. Leaders in the Church of England have traditionally been paid, but now there are a number of unpaid clergy known as 'non-stipendiary ministers' who are either employed in a secular job or have retired from that job. Among the Brethren there has traditionally been a refusal to employ salaried ministers, though there have been a number of itinerant teachers living 'by faith' from donations. Now a number of Brethren assemblies have paid 'workers' as teachers or evangelists.

**5. Leadership is to be both settled and mobile**

The list of leaders in Ephesians 4 includes pastors and teachers who were presumably the settled elders of a local

church. The apostles, prophets and evangelists would have
travelled more widely. Again it is unwise to assume a rigid
distinction. Agabus and his group of prophets moved from
place to place (Acts 11:27–28; 21:10) but so did some
teachers (Acts 15:1). During the persecution at Jerusalem
the apostles stayed put, while the others moved out (Acts
8:1). Then some of the apostles began to travel and we find
Peter at Lydda and Joppa, and then Caesarea (Acts 9 and
10). The distinction between settled and mobile is an
important one, for it shows that there is a place for those
who exercise a mobile ministry, and such a ministry can
prevent the local church from becoming too inward looking
and eventually moribund. Mobile leaders are in any case
needed in order to found new churches. The most famous
example is the sending out of Paul and Barnabas from the
church at Antioch (Acts 13:1). Throughout the following
centuries the settled church experienced a variety of movements bringing a new vision of renewal and mission.
Examples include the monastic and Franciscan movements, Methodism which was originally a movement within
the Church of England, and the nineteenth-century
missionary societies. As a general criticism the western
church has become too settled and pastoral and not sufficiently mobile and missionary. We need mobile leaders
with the gifts of evangelism and church planting, not only
'microphone evangelists' but also those who can visit local
churches in order to equip and train others for the work of
evangelism.

## 6. Leaders are to be servants

The pattern set by Jesus is that of the servant, just as the
Messiah is foretold as a servant in Isaiah. 'You know that
those who are regarded as rulers of the Gentiles lord it over
them. . . . Not so with you. Instead whoever wants to be
great among you must be your servant. . . . For even the
Son of Man did not come to be served, but to serve' (Mark
10:42–5). St Peter writes: 'To the elders among you,

I appeal as a fellow elder. . . . Be shepherds of God's flock . . . not greedy for money, but eager to serve; not lording it over those entrusted to you, but being examples to the flock' (1 Peter 5:1–3). There is no place for autocratic leadership in the church of God. Jesus sets the pattern of the servant in his leadership, and we shall see some of the implications of this in Chapter 9.

## 7. Leaders include both men and women

The question of whether to ordain women as priests, presbyters or elders is being hotly debated and some members of the Church of England have threatened to separate if such a move is taken. The question illustrates well the problem of discovering blueprints for leadership in the New Testament and of discerning whether commands and practices are temporary and local or permanent and universal. The twelve apostles were all men, but it could be argued that Jesus felt it wise to avoid unnecessary controversy by observing the conventions of his day. Jewish women had a subordinate position both in society and in the synagogue. A new synagogue could not be founded unless there were at least ten men present, however many the number of women, thus demonstrating that in every sense a woman did not count. Jesus went a long way to raise the status of women and they were included in the wider group of his disciples, were the first witnesses of his resurrection and were among the fellowship of believers who first experienced Pentecost. Both male and female together received the authority, power and gifts of the Spirit to further Christ's mission. Jesus in fact restricted the apostles to male Jews and if women are to be excluded from leadership today on this basis, so should male Gentiles; in any case elders or presbyters are not directly descended from the apostles. Emphasis has been laid by some opponents of women's ordination on three passages which seem to explicitly deny leadership roles to women; they are 1 Corinthians 11:2–16, 1 Corinthians 14:34–6 and 1 Timothy

2:8–15. The last passage is perhaps the most difficult for it expressly states, 'I do not permit a woman to teach or to have authority over a man; she must be silent. For Adam was formed first, then Eve' (1 Timothy 2:12–13). Some have argued in defence that this applies solely to married women in their relationship to their husbands, while others argue that it is simply a temporary local command because of the position of women in society at that time. There is a possible parallel with slavery as a radical attack on the position of slaves or women would have created too much opposition. It is true that the command seems to have a permanent application in that it is linked to Adam and Eve and the relationship of man and woman at creation, but Paul makes a similar link in 1 Corinthians 11 when giving advice about haircuts and headcoverings (vv 4–10); logically those who forbid women to teach in church on these grounds should also forbid men to have long hair.

These difficult passages need to be interpreted in harmony with the Bible as a whole. In Genesis 1 man is male and female and both sexes have an equal relationship to God and an equal responsibility as stewards of God's creation (Genesis 1:27–8). It is true that the Fall recorded in Genesis 3 resulted in a tendency to male domination (v 16), but Christ came to reverse the result of the Fall and to restore creation, so that in him Jew and Greek, slave and free, male and female become one (Galatians 3:28). Within marriage it is still possible to talk about male headship, provided that we see it as a redeemed headship that has the hallmark of sacrificial love (Ephesians 5:22–5). But marriage is an institution for this life alone, while the church is the first-fruits of a kingdom that lasts for eternity, so it does not follow that the church's ministry must necessarily be exercised under male headship. When we come to look at the individuals Paul lists in Romans 16 we see Phoebe described as a deacon (v 1),[8] Mary as someone who has 'worked hard' (v 6) and Junias as an 'apostle' (v 7), though it has to be said that 'Junias' could be a man's name. It is interesting to see Priscilla's name (v 3) coming before her husband's; they were both notable for correcting the theology of Apollos (Acts 18:24–6) but it seems that Priscilla took the lead. Certainly women are in the forefront of those Paul mentions. There is little doubt that there were female deacons in the early church and no doubt that there were female prophets and evangelists so it seems very likely that there were female elders, too, though the case is not proven.

A narrow and permanent interpretation of 1 Timothy 2:8–15 rules out women from any public teaching ministry, but some take a midway position and see the verses as prohibiting women from having a position of final authority; in the Church of England this would not rule out women priests, but it might rule out women incumbents and certainly women bishops. It must be admitted that this and other passages are open to more than one interpretation, but it is difficult to deny that women shared in leadership roles through evangelism, prophecy and some forms of teaching. Throughout this book, therefore, it may be assumed that any reference to leadership envisages both men and women.[9]

# 4 ASKING QUESTIONS

The need to analyse styles of leadership and
to ask which is appropriate according to –

the area
others' expectations
the stage of development
the task in hand
our gifts

Distinctions between consultant, organising
and administrative leadership

We have seen that the New Testament does not give a precise blueprint for leadership, but it does give a number of guidelines and principles which provide us with a general blueprint. Leadership is to be shared, and one of its goals must be to equip others for ministry. It is to be varied, flexible and both settled and mobile. Above all, leaders are to be servants. In applying these principles, however, there is a good deal of room for different styles and approaches. There will be occasions when a more charismatic style is appropriate and others when it is not. All too often leaders assume that only one style is right and that is usually the one most suited to their personality. Some are too insecure to ask questions about the style they have adopted. In order to achieve a leadership explosion leaders must be ready to analyse their type of leadership, with its strengths and weaknesses, and to recognise that there are advantages in other types. The first step towards effective leadership is to be ready to ask questions about styles, methods and structures. 'In a real sense the Bible is not an answer book, but a question book. Asking the right questions within the context of the situation is usually the most important thing we can do.'[1]

The first question is –

*What style of leadership is most appropriate in our area?*

In an area where there are strong-minded, articulate professionals the leadership will need to be able to give clear direction without being autocratic. In order to argue the case for change it may be necessary to produce one or several papers, to set up a working party or to send a study group to visit other churches to see how the idea works in practice. In an Urban Priority Area the situation may be different. There may be vocal leaders from a trade union background, but in other cases the congregation may consist in the main of those who are diffident at taking a lead, however much they grumble once the meeting is over. In these cases it will be possible to take a strong lead and effect rapid changes without generating open opposition, and it will be tempting to do so. Peter Wagner, writing from the North American scene, says, 'Factory workers respond well to authoritative type leadership . . . Working-class people for the most part do not care to be part of the decision-making process. They feel uncomfortable if they are expected to come up with ideas. They are used to the foreman or the union boss telling them what to do, and they do not resent it in the least.'[2] Wagner may be exaggerating to make a point, but if we take his recommendations at their face value they could be a recipe for short-term gain at the expense of long-term disaster. If our goal is simply to increase the size of the congregation authoritarian leadership can produce success. But true church growth is a matter of quality as well as quantity; our goals must include the objective of developing the character, gifts and skills of every member and this in turn will lead to a leadership

explosion and to church growth in every sense. In an Urban
Priority Area it is essential to have the kind of leadership
that encourages others to take decisions, rather than auto-
cratically riding roughshod over them. The fact that some
are not used to taking part in decisions at work is an
argument for them doing so in church life, not the opposite.
Otherwise we deny them the opportunity of full development as sons of God, born and reborn in his image. In any
case people 'own' and support a programme when they
have had a hand in shaping it. The minister who complains
that he can never find volunteers to help may have never
shared the planning of the programme with others. A
refusal to take seriously the need to develop local leadership is one of the main reasons for the church's failure in
Urban Priority Areas.

The second question to ask is –

## What style is expected?

The minister who follows an autocratic leader cannot im-
mediately change the approach without a congregation
feeling bewildered, insecure and threatened. Peter Rudge
quotes the case of a Church of England bishop who tried to
change the nature of his diocese from a classical to a more
democratic model. 'In many areas of diocesan life there
was uncertainty as to the way to go; people were not used
to making, or able to make, the necessary decisions
themselves.'[3] This does not mean that changes in style are
to be avoided but simply that they must be made with care.
A new leader needs to be aware of the approaches used in
the past and therefore of other people's expectations. If a
'strong lead' is expected it may be necessary to give one in
the early stages and then prepare the ground for a more
open and democratic approach.

In the process of change the leader may find his ability to
lead is called into question and his confidence undermined;
he will need to remind himself that really 'strong' leadership is the ability to stand back and let others develop their

leadership skills even if they make mistakes in doing so. Careful preparation and training will be needed. Those who have learnt to submit to autocratic leaders are usually dependent by nature or have learnt to be so. In order to prepare for shared leadership the new minister may need to take his church committee away for a conference or retreat. By getting away from the routine of a normal business meeting it is possible to look at issues in a more relaxed, unhurried way. Dividing into discussion groups will help those not used to discussion and debate. Following the conference he may want to set up study groups and eventually task groups to turn discussion into action. These procedures are, of course, valuable whether or not there has been autocratic leadership in the past.

Whatever style is thought to be appropriate it is vital to note what approach has been used hitherto and to know what is common in society around.

The third question is –

*What style is appropriate at this stage of development?*

The Christian leader will want to encourage others to participate in planning, but what if a majority of church members are not yet spiritually mature? At an early stage of development a stronger lead will need to be taken by the minister or group of elders, and a totally democratic approach could lead to disastrous consequences. A large gathering can more easily be dominated by the vocal few and they are not always the most spiritually mature. In order to give a clear lead without being autocratic it may be best to initiate planning with a smaller standing committee or group of elders; the programme can then be presented to the church committee or to the church meeting for discussion and final decision.

In Acts 15 we have an instructive example of how the early church dealt with the vital question of whether Gentile converts should be expected to keep Jewish laws. First the apostles and elders meet to consider the question, and then Peter stands up to share his experience and conviction. The whole assembly listen to Paul and Barnabas recounting the signs and wonders they had seen among the Gentiles. Then James gives his judgment and the final decision is made or ratified by 'the apostles and elders, with the whole church'. It is difficult to be sure of all the details, including the question of whether the whole church was present throughout, and it would be unwise to draw from this chapter mandatory guidelines for all times and all places. However, it is an interesting illustration of the interplay between individual leaders, the group of elders and the whole church.[4]

The fourth question is –

## *What style is appropriate for this task?*

As we saw in Chapter 1 the human relations style is the most appropriate for small group discussion. In the strictly controlled group the lines of discussion run towards and away from the leader. In the more developed group the leader becomes a catalyst to enable members of the group to interact with each other. (See the diagram overleaf.) Even here the task will determine the style. If it is a

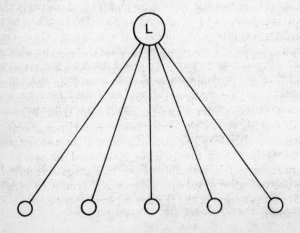

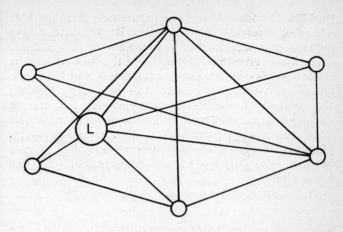

beginners' teaching group the leader may dominate more, though he will still want to draw out the feelings and experience of all those present. If there is a member of the awkward squad present the leader will again need to keep stricter control.

At the other extreme, in a large meeting, celebration or congregation a more charismatic style will be needed, though even here it is good to give opportunity for others to be trained up and equipped for platform ministry. I well remember a visit to a large and famous Baptist church where the pastor conducted the whole ninety-minute service and preached. The only other person allowed on the platform was the church secretary who gave out the notices.

Similarly leadership styles may have to be different in the task of looking after a large congregation than is the case with a smaller one. The minister may need lines of defence such as a secretary, an Ansaphone and an appointments system. If this is the case he will need to create the impression that he is readily available in cases of emergency and he will need to set up a system of shared leadership so that access to one of the leaders is possible for each church member.

There may arise issues which the minister feels unable to put to the vote because, in his mind, they are matters of conscience or of clear biblical principle. The Brownies may want to 'guess the weight of the cake' as opposed to estimating it, or the Scouts may want to launch a football pool to raise funds, but the minister is opposed to every form of gambling. Even where the minister feels the issue is of such clear principle that there is no question for debate, persuasion and discussion are better than riding roughshod over others, as we saw in Acts 15. The minister who makes rapid and sweeping changes in worship with the words 'we must follow New Testament principle' or 'the conduct of worship is my prerogative,' for example, is making short-term gains at the expense of long-term losses.

The final and most important question is –

## What style is appropriate for my (or our) gifts?

Some have personalities and gifts that are particularly suited for charismatic leadership in a pioneer setting, while others have human relations skills that equip them for being effective team members in a more developed setting. It is clear from 1 Corinthians 12 that Christians are given a variety of gifts and that no Christian, not even a minister, has all the gifts. One of the arguments for shared leadership is that a group of leaders can share the necessary leadership tasks among them.

We have, of course, to take care in answering the question 'What style is appropriate for my gifts?' We may already have latent gifts that have not been recognised or exercised, or the Lord may grant us new gifts for new tasks, as seems to have happened with Timothy; Paul says to him, 'For this reason I remind you to fan into flame the gift of God, which is in you through the laying on of my hands' (2 Timothy 1:6).

## Consultant and organising leadership

A useful distinction can be made between consultant leadership and organising leadership. For purposes of definition organisers are those who have the gift of rallying people to a common task. They have the ability to collect together a team and mobilise them to achieve certain goals.

Sadly, a disturbing number of those who emerge from theological colleges do not have the gifts either of organising or of administration, though they are usually put into positions where organising gifts are expected of them. Perhaps we should not expect this of them. Their training does not usually include organisation and administration. Furthermore, those ordained in their mid-twenties may not have had the opportunity of discovering whether they have these gifts.

For this reason it may not be right for the minister to be chairman of committees or to be seen as the organiser. In one growing charismatic church I visited, the vicar had been set apart to concentrate on prayer and counselling. He spent considerable time in seeking the Lord's vision for the way ahead. He certainly gave a lead to the church, but the organising leadership was left to another full-time staff member. Would that others had the courage to take on a role suited to their gifts rather than become a square peg in the round hole of other people's expectations. Dr Michael Griffiths, Principal of London Bible College, has said, 'The traditional view of the vicar as an equally gifted preacher, pastor and organiser was humbug; the number who excel in all three areas is very small. I see occasional references . . . to the idea that he is still the natural chairman and leader. One could question even this. He might be a superb teacher or pastor who should delegate the role of organising leader to another.'[5]

We saw in Chapter 2 that Roman Catholic base communities usually have a local lay leader and the priest is brought in as a consultant; his is a consulting leadership rather than an organising leadership. John Tiller has made

use of this idea in recommending a radical restructuring of
the Church of England's leadership ministry: 'There is no
compelling reason why the role of (liturgical) president,
chairman and pastor should be combined.'[6] The implication is that the ordained minister should be set apart as
consultant or teacher, leaving others to do the organising.
Tiller's scheme goes wider than the local church and sees
certain ordained ministers as belonging to a diocesan team.
To give an over-simplified summary of the proposals, the
scheme is to encourage local leaders to emerge in each
parish church, taking on the responsibility for organisation
and pastoral care. The local leaders are serviced by full-
time staff who cover a wider area and provide mission and
teaching skills. The Tiller scheme picks up many of the New
Testament leadership principles spelt out in Chapter 3.
Whether it is too radical to win acceptance in a church
whose structures are very different remains to be seen. It
may eventually be accepted from economic pressure rather
than from principle, just as the new emphasis on the
ministry of the laity came mainly because of a growing
shortage of clergy, rather than from principle.[7]

## Organising and administrative leadership

Not only is it useful to distinguish between 'organisers' and
'consultants', it is also useful to distinguish between 'organisers' and 'administrators'. Organisers mobilise a team
to achieve certain goals, while administrators give the
detailed administrative back-up to make the whole organisation work smoothly. Some organisers are not good
administrators. Paul uses the interesting word 'kubernesis'
in 1 Corinthians 12:28. It literally means a steersman or
pilot, one who directs the whole ship. 'God has put all in
place – in the first place apostles . . . followed by those who
are given the power to . . . help others or to direct them' (1
Corinthians 12:28 GNB).[8] David Prior comments, 'Let us
carefully protect the helmsman from the burdens of administration – a task which is far better accomplished by those

whom Paul calls "helpers" . . . the Body of Christ will become hard and crusty without pastoral care and wise, sensitive helmsmanship. Equally it will become chaotic and slipshod without efficient administration.'[9] The pilot or steersman has already charted out the waters ahead, he knows the direction in which the ship should go, and he organises the crew so as to keep the ship on course. This is a lovely picture of the organising leader.

It is vital that all ministers and leaders, whether ordained or not, ask searching questions about their gifts and the appropriate style of leadership for each situation. Ideally ministers will not ask these questions on their own, but will share them with a group of mature church members. Dr Michael Griffiths observes,

There ought to be a wider recognition that we need pastors and teachers and administrators and a person in training should be told where his gifts lie. It is not failure to be a pastor but not a teacher, but he must be told this while he is still at college, by his first incumbent and throughout his ministry by his bishop. At all times there must be someone in authority who can tell him this so that he can supplement his weaknesses with the strengths of others. This has many implications for ministerial selection and training.[10]

# Part II

# The Practice of Leadership

# 5  SHARED LEADERSHIP

Shared leadership in the early church

The need for a leadership explosion in contexts of growth and decline

The mutual support and enrichment of a team

Team building as part of the church's task

Involvement and motivation

Team building as the key to expansion

So far we have talked mainly of the leader or the minister in the singular, but as we have seen, New Testament leaders are nearly always in the plural. Leadership in the early church is shared leadership, making possible a rapid leadership explosion.

It might be assumed that Jesus had all the gifts necessary for an effective all-round ministry, yet he chose not to work on his own. Right at the beginning he selected twelve to share not only his ministry but his life. They were a mixed, often quarrelsome group, at times slow to learn and prone to misunderstanding and it must have tried his patience to sort out their misunderstandings and their squabbles. Their presence in human terms had a crippling effect. One was to deny him and another to betray him. Yet he deliberately demonstrated a model of shared leadership.

Similarly the leaders in the early church selected others

to share in their work of evangelism and teaching. The apostle Paul was selected and trained through shared leadership. Barnabas introduced him to the church at Jerusalem, eased him into the fellowship there and helped him to gain acceptance (Acts 9:27) in spite of the disciples' very natural suspicions. Later Barnabas became engaged in a very demanding ministry at Antioch. Rather than become a workaholic or suffer a breakdown he went to Tarsus to look for Paul and brought him to Antioch. For a while they had a shared teaching ministry (Acts 11:19–26) and later the two were sent out from Antioch as missionaries. Barnabas' name was an appropriate one, meaning 'son of encouragement'. There is probably no more important quality to look for in those called to train others for leadership than the gift of encouragement; many who are in leadership positions today are there because at an early stage they were given opportunity and encouragement to develop their gifts.

Shared leadership can, however, run into problems. Barnabas and Paul eventually quarrelled over the suitability of one of their team, a man named Mark, and their quarrel led to a split. Nevertheless they both continued the principle of shared leadership, Barnabas taking Mark and Paul taking Silas (Acts 15:36–40). Together Paul and Silas visited the churches planted earlier and they were joined by Timothy at Lystra and by Luke at Troas. This team shared in preaching and church planting at Philippi, Thessalonica, Berea and Corinth. Silas co-operated with Paul in writing 1 and 2 Thessalonians and Timothy was associated with him in six of his letters.

This same principle was urged on the Church of England by its Partners in Mission Consultation held in 1981. 'The clergy should be selected and trained for a ministry which is always shared with others.'[1] Many years before Hans-Ruedi Weber had argued, 'The laity are not the helpers of the clergy so that the clergy can do their job, but the clergy are helpers of the whole people of God so that the laity can be the church.'[2]

Why is shared leadership so important? There are at least five reasons –

*The situation needs it*

It is impossible for one minister to visit every home in an area, unless it is a rural one, or to counsel all those who need help, let alone take up every opportunity for evangelism and witness. It was D. L. Moody who said, 'I would rather put ten men to work than do the work of ten men.'[3] In most denominations the number of 'full-time' salaried ministers is declining and the only answer is to build up teams of non-professional leaders. In general church membership rolls are falling but there are many congregations where growth is taking place; in these cases shared leadership is vital in order not to lose opportunities. Luke describes an occasion when Simon was urged, 'Put out into deep water and let down the nets for a catch.' The result was such a large number of fish that their nets began to break. Instead of giving up in despair, 'They signalled their partners in the other boat to come and help them' (Luke 5:4 and 7). A church in the North of England described how growth had led to a number of 'traffic jams'. There were new members needing to be taught the basics of the Christian faith, house groups had increased in number and leaders needed training and support, while individuals and couples were increasingly looking for counselling in personal and emotional problems. At the same time there was a decrease in the number of clergy while a renewed emphasis on the ministry and gifts of the Holy Spirit had produced a growing number of laity anxious to serve. The pressure could only be released by taking the cork out of the bottle, creating a team and allowing for a leadership explosion.

It was fascinating to visit St Andrew's Cathedral in Sydney for one of their mid-week healing services. The cathedral was packed with the crowds who had come to hear instruction and receive healing. At the end of the

service it would have been impossible for the leader to
minister personally to everyone. Instead those who wanted
help raised a hand and trained counsellors came alongside.
If shared leadership can widen the ministry in a cathedral
how much more could it do so throughout a city?

### The leaders need it

'Whenever I made decisions on my own,' said the vicar of a
busy inner city church, 'the Lord allowed me to make
mistakes.' Every vision needs checking, every idea benefits
from comment and we all need support, encouragement
and correction. Each individual is limited in his or her gifts
and experience and needs both balancing and com-
plementing by others. Mutual support is particularly important in a pioneer situation, such as an inner city church
or a new housing estate. Too often a new minister is
allowed to find his feet on his own. If economic factors
make it impossible to send in more than one ordained
minister then several lay families should be encouraged
to move home into the area and give support. Patrick
Sookhdeo has suggested in East London, 'A deployment of
personnel in certain key areas in the urban context, not just
one person, one couple, but maybe two or three couples
each with different gifts to create new things'.[4]

Urban church planting in South America has been far
more effective when teams rather than isolated couples
have been deployed. Church planting is a process that
begins with evangelism and ends with the formation of a
church that is self-supporting, self-governing and self-
propagating. Ideally a church planting team will include at
least one with the gift of an evangelist and one with the gift
of being a pastor and teacher so that new converts can
straightaway be incorporated into a new congregation.
Wherever possible the teams include Latin Americans as
well as missionaries, just as teams in urban Britain ideally
include locals as well as 'outsiders'.

Jesus chose as leaders a very mixed group. The twelve

included a tax-collector, Matthew, who had been prepared to work with the hated Roman government and so would have been regarded by some as a traitor or quisling; at the other end of the political spectrum was Simon the Zealot or revolutionary. Peter and Andrew might have been from a slightly lower social group than James and John whose father had hired servants in his boat. Shared leadership can provide a mix of insights, convictions and backgrounds. I have been encouraged, helped and enriched by working in different teams over the years. These have included charismatics and non-charismatics, visionaries who are quick to run off in new directions, more pedestrian friends who bring solid reliability as a gift to the team, those with radical political views and those who are more traditional. The visionary will bring excitement, vigour and a host of new ideas, while the more cautious team members will filter, evaluate and implement. Visionaries may not be good at implementation and their enthusiasm may make them blind to the practical problems to be overcome, while those who are skilled at implementing may fail to see the wood for the trees. It is vital, of course, that members of a team develop an openness that frees them to express their own convictions and enables them to respect the personalities and the views of others. It has been well said that a mixed team can provide creativity, commitment and conflict. A team that never experiences conflict is unlikely to be a creative one.

Relationships between leaders are not always easy, as we saw with Barnabas and Paul. One of the biggest difficulties for missionaries overseas, for example, is not so much the bugs, the heat or the snakes, but relationships with others. David Watson has said, 'Personal friendships need to be formed at the leadership level, since it is often here that the barriers are strongest, perhaps because of professional jealousy or the feelings of being threatened.' He quotes the German philosopher Schopenhauer as saying that people are rather like a pack of porcupines on a freezing winter night. 'The sub-zero temperature forces them together for warmth. But as soon as they press very close they jab and hurt one another.'[5] But when leaders with very different personalities and backgrounds are able to work together they become a living symbol of the new community that God wants to plant. The Gospel is then proclaimed by life as well as by word.

### Developing leaders and ministers is part of the church's task

In industry there is often a tension between increasing profits and being concerned for the welfare of employees. A Christian who applied for a job in the welfare department of a large company some years ago was firmly told, 'The goal of the welfare department is the same as that of the company – the maximisation of profit. There can only be a concern for welfare if it is part of this overall aim.' Management theory has changed considerably since then, partly because it has been demonstrated that a concern for people is integral to the effectiveness of a company. The one quoted above has slowly shrunk. Recent research into the top ten successful companies in the United States has shown that people-orientation is the main key to their success.[6] They listened to their employees and treated them as adults. 'People are our most important asset,' said one spokesman.[7] The two different management emphases are often shown as a grid, where the horizontal line represents a concern for production and the vertical line a concern for people.

In the early days of church growth theory the impression was sometimes given that the goal of achieving growth in numbers was so overriding that the welfare of individuals hardly mattered (point 9.1 on the grid). The weak and ineffective in society could be left on one side if others were more responsive, and autocratic leadership could be justified if it increased the production of converts. Today there is a healthier emphasis on quality of growth as well as quantity and the development of shared leadership is seen

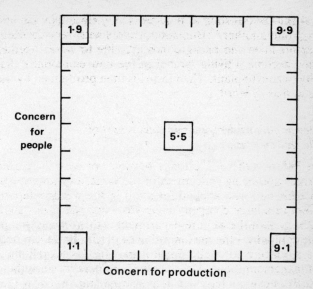

Companies which emphasise profits to the exclusion of people will be found at point 9.1; not only are they likely to be impersonal and ruthless, they are also likely in the long run to be unsuccessful. At the opposite extreme are companies at point 1.9 which are so immersed in welfare programmes that they fail to pay sufficient attention to production; they are sometimes described as 'country clubs'. In church life we would describe 1.9 as 'human relations' leadership which is concerned for people but has no goals for growth. The successful companies are concerned with both people and production and are found at point 9.9.

as one of the keys to growth in all dimensions. In management terms part of our production task is producing new people. Paul described his aim in Colossians 1 as follows: 'We proclaim him, admonishing and teaching everyone with all wisdom, so that we may present everyone perfect in Christ. To this end I labour, struggling with all his energy, which so powerfully works in me' (vv 28–9).

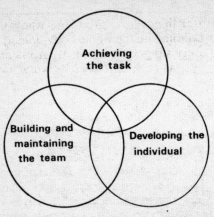

But the need to achieve the task and to develop individuals has to be balanced by the need to build a leadership team. John Adair has suggested three intersecting circles as providing a triple goal for leaders in industry – developing the individual, building and maintaining the team and achieving the task.[8] This triple goal is appropriate for the church as well.

Juan Carlos Ortiz, the Argentine Pentecostal leader, has accused professional ministers of behaving like night-watchmen guarding a pile of bricks, when they should be builders integrating the bricks together to form a temple.[9] The same is true of leaders; they have to be built into a team that will be effective in training others for ministry. There are parallels with coaching a sports team where players have different positions and skills but have to learn not to play as isolated individuals. Success depends on recognising complementary roles, creating opportunities for others and backing them up as they take them.

The goal of both shared ministry and shared leadership is described in Ephesians 4. 'To prepare God's people for works of service, so that the body of Christ may be built up until we all reach unity in the faith and in the knowledge of the Son of God and become mature, attaining to the whole measure of the fulness of Christ . . . speaking the truth in love, we will in all things grow up into him who is the Head, that is, Christ. From him the whole body, joined and held together by every supporting ligament, grows and builds itself up in love, as each part does its work' (vv 12–13, 15–16).

## People are motivated by becoming involved

Field-Marshal Montgomery's advice was to 'make men partners'. The secret of successful leadership is to help others to see their part in making the master plan a success or failure.[10] The top ten companies quoted above have exploded the myth that employees are only motivated by money. The success of these companies lies in the fact that 'by offering meaning as well as money they give their employees a mission as well as a sense of feeling great'.[11] By consulting as widely as possible and involving others in the process of decision-making the whole church can be motivated to 'own' the goals and the programme of its leadership. It is salutary to observe churches where there have been rapid changes in worship, structures or programme without adequate consultation or with only a pretence at consultation. At the first stage there seem to be good results, but soon many of the congregation begin to grumble and then become alienated. They do not feel involved and so are unwilling to volunteer for tasks. Eventually the leaders themselves grumble, 'We are always left to do everything; no-one seems to be ready to help.' In this kind of church, disputes seem to arise over trifling issues. The reason for this is highlighted by J. Northcote Parkinson in his famous book *Parkinson's Law or the Pursuit of Progress*: 'The man who is denied the opportunity of taking decisions of importance begins to regard as important the decisions he is allowed to take.'[12] As a result church committee agendas become dominated by drains, flower arrangements and the autumn fair and arguments arise over peripheral matters.

*Shared leadership is essential for expansion*

Frank Woolworth found that his firm began to grow as soon as he was ready to share leadership with others. 'I lost my conceit that nobody could do anything as well as I could. So long as I had the idea that I must attend personally to everything large-scale operation was impossible.'[13] Churches which are growing both in quality and quantity are those where the professional minister is sharing the task of evangelism, teaching and counselling, and where others are being trained to conduct marriage and baptism preparation.

In the diagram the nine outer circles represent nine leadership groups each with different tasks and functions.

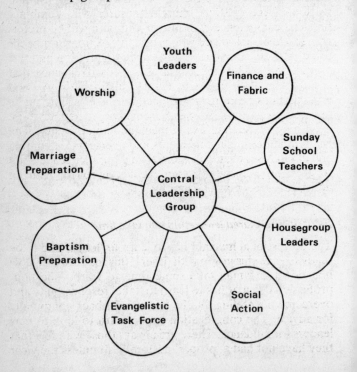

They are only samples; others could be added or substituted. The leader of each leadership group is also a member of the central group.

There are, however, a number of warnings to be observed in setting up a shared leadership –

## Careful selection is needed

Care and prayer are essential preliminaries before a choice is made. Jesus spent all night in prayer before choosing the twelve (Luke 6:12–13). Spiritual qualities are essential even for administrative tasks; those chosen to 'wait on tables' were nevertheless to be 'full of the Spirit and wisdom' (Acts 6:3). A church treasurer who combines financial competence with prayer and faith will be preferable to a financial wizard who lacks faith. A treasurer needs to be methodical and cautious, ready to question and test every ambitious scheme, but he also needs to recognise that a church is often called to launch out in faith. A good administrator needs to be businesslike and efficient, but he also needs a pastoral heart and a sensitivity to people; there is nothing worse than a cold machine-like efficiency. The list of qualities in pastoral elders and overseers is daunting and emphasises character more than gifts; such leaders are to be gentle, hospitable, and above reproach, with an aptitude for teaching (1 Timothy 3:1–7).

## Establishing shared leadership can take time

The professional minister has to learn to 'let go' and to be ready to share his vision with others; this may initially slow him down and may take some time to learn. The non-professional leader has to learn to 'take' responsibility and overcome the feeling that he has to refer back continually for advice. The congregation has to learn to look to new leaders for guidance. There are always those who feel that they have not had a 'proper' pastoral visit unless the vicar calls in person, and there will be those who feel they have not been 'properly' prepared for baptism, confirmation or marriage unless the preparation has been done by the professional clergy. Establishing shared leadership can not only take time, but will also be time-consuming. A vicar in the North of England commented, 'I learned early on that the group had to be number one priority for me. I am not available on Pastoral Leadership evenings except in emergencies. This sets the tone for everyone else. I lead the group but am also subject to them.'

## Shared leadership can be demanding

Those who earn their living as car mechanics, postmen, doctors and directors cannot possibly give as much time as they would like to leadership tasks within the church. This has to be recognised and those within the leadership team released from other tasks as much as possible. In one parish the whole elders' scheme had to be abandoned because those involved found the burdens too great. In any case it would be tragic if those who have opportunities of leadership in the world of work find their energy sapped through a round of parochial meetings. It is essential that ministry is shared outside the leadership team as well as inside in order to avoid 'core group burn out'.

## Sharing needs to take place in ever-widening circles

The ministry of Jesus was shared in ever widening circles. On the Mount of Transfiguration and in the Garden of Gethsemane Jesus took with him just Peter, James and John (Matthew 17:1 and 26:37). More often all twelve apostles were included. At one point he commissioned seventy (Luke 10:1) and frequently he ministered to large crowds.

It is possible for the one-man bottleneck to be simply replaced by a five-person bottleneck, and a team can be as distanced from the congregation as an individual can. This

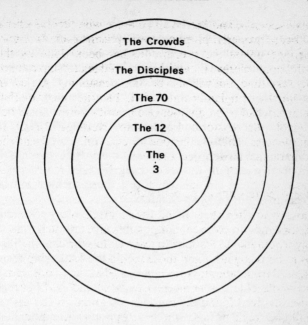

The Crowds

The Disciples

The 70

The 12

The
3

is a danger when there is a 'team' of full-time professionals ministering to a number of churches.[14] It is also a danger when a single congregation has a full-time staff team. Dr Michael Griffiths has said, 'We must not repeat the mistake of the American pattern where a large number of specialist staff does more and more and the congregation do less and less.'[15] On one occasion I was preaching in a church in the States and found that they had a full-time staff of forty, including fourteen clergy; there was little evidence that the congregation as a whole were being mobilised for ministry and mission. Unwillingness to share leadership and ministry is not a fault that is limited to the full-time professional; a man who is in a subordinate position at work may value a position of authority in the church for the wrong reasons, and may want to bolster that position by refusing to share leadership with others. The eldership team and the church council or committee have to be careful not to become viewed as an inward looking secretive clique. This danger can be overcome by giving all church members regular opportunities for open discussion. In many churches this is only provided at an annual meeting of members and often the agenda is so formalised that open discussion is discouraged. When the early church met together the time seems to have been spent in discussion and debate as well as in worship and teaching.

Sharing of leadership is a skill that needs developing. It will involve learning the art of delegation and may necessitate changes in church structures; these themes will be taken up in the next two chapters.

# 6   DELEGATION

## Initiating a leadership explosion

*Seven aspects of delegation*

Selection

Job description

Authority and responsibility

Objectives

Training

Support

Reporting back

Professional ministers fall into one of five categories:
   those who never or rarely delegate;
   those who delegate without giving adequate training;
   those who establish training schemes, but fail to give those trained a specific job once the training period is over;
   those who delegate responsibility, but then take all or part of the responsibility back again;
   others who have successfully developed the art of delegation.
   Those in the first category bemoan the fact that they cannot delegate because there is no one capable to do the task in hand. But whose fault is it if there is no one adequately trained or prepared? Ian Smith used to argue

against universal democracy in Rhodesia on the grounds that black Africans were not educated or sophisticated enough to exercise a vote, but whose fault was their lack of education? The minister quoted in our Introduction came in this category: 'I keep committee meetings brief. Most members know very little about the subjects being discussed.' Whose fault was their ignorance?

The second category – delegation without proper training – is really abdication not delegation. How often a church member is asked to take over the youth club, the Sunday school or a housegroup without being given the opportunity of a training course or even of being an understudy before the present leader retires. John Stott wrote in 1969: 'I myself have only recently learned that the true art of delegation is not to hand over work to somebody else and then forget about it, but to commit work to a deputy who knows that he is responsible to you and can at times report back and seek advice.'[1]

The third category is that of training without responsibility. Many fall into the trap of preparing training courses on evangelism or pastoral care without working out a programme in advance so that those trained can use their experience to good effect. Such a training course then becomes a substitute for action rather than a stimulus to it. A comprehensive training programme for ministry has been developed in South America under the title of SEAN,[2] where students are given opportunity for ministry as they train and so learn by doing. It has been translated into English and used with significant success in a large number of British churches, but in several instances those trained have been frustrated because they have not been given opportunities to exercise their ministry.

The ministry of Jesus gives us a model of effective delegation. He took the twelve with him as he engaged in evangelism, teaching and healing throughout Galilee and Judea. He demonstrated how to do it, and he delegated specific tasks to the twelve and later to the seventy. With delegation came authority and responsibility (Luke 9:1–6;

10:1–24). The disciples would come back to Jesus to discuss their ministry and to share both success and difficulties. Demonstration and delegation were followed by discussion; action was interwoven with reflection and followed by further teaching.

While Jesus was on the Mount of Transfiguration with Peter, James and John, the other disciples tried to heal a boy who was possessed by a demon. They failed. 'Why couldn't we drive it out?' they asked Jesus. 'Because you have so little faith' (Matthew 17:19–20). Jesus then used the occasion to give further teaching on the nature and application of faith. Teaching is always more compelling and memorable when it relates to issues that are currently being faced. This is the value of action interwoven with reflection. 'Vicar,' said one parishioner, 'I've just been visited by a Jehovah's Witness. Could we have a sermon series about them?' 'I didn't like to tell her', confessed the vicar afterwards, 'that we had one last year.' A professional minister in East Anglia explained that he set the following goal: 'I never exercise ministry on my own unless I have to. Wherever possible I bring others alongside to share it with me.' If he went on a visit he took a member of the congregation along with him. If he ran a baptism preparation class he made sure he had one or two experienced Christian couples sharing in it. Later he would delegate the visiting, the classes or the follow-up to others.

It is useful to separate out seven dimensions of successful delegation:

Select carefully;
Describe the task;
Define the authority and responsibility;
Discuss the objectives;
Arrange the training;
Provide the support;
Plan a reporting system.

**Select carefully**

Selection has been mentioned on page 81. Sometimes it may be better to leave a task undone rather than appoint someone who is unsuitable. Careful advance planning and a system of understudies avoids the last minute panic that forces square pegs into round holes. Ideally the central leadership group will keep each section of church life under review in order to spot the needs. It is also valuable to discuss the church membership list, taking one section a month, in order to monitor each individual's growth, to identify their gifts and to find ways of encouraging the development of their ministry. In larger churches this task has to be delegated to area or sector leadership groups, as described in Chapter 7.


**Describe the task**

After three years in a new job a church worker complained, 'The lack of a clear job description has led to frustration and this has not been helped by the fact that there has not been any clear leading from the vicar as to what he expects of me.' She was unsure whether her ministry was being valued and as a result lacked confidence and job satisfaction. It seems incredible that such a breakdown in communication can occur, but it is not uncommon. It is a growing practice to issue detailed, written job descriptions, describing the task, the objectives and the lines of authority and responsibility. A written job description may be unnecessary for the majority of tasks in a local church, but whether or not they are written down, the nature, aims and objectives of the task need to be made clear. Before a Sunday school teacher is appointed, for example, it is wise to outline what the job entails. No doubt the teacher is expected to spend time on preparation, but what about a regular teachers' meeting, church attendance, training courses, visits to parents, joining in outings and helping in the annual holiday club? It is better to describe the expectations before the teacher starts even if he feels unable to fulfil them all.

## Define the authority and responsibility

Two missionaries working in the same village were having relationship problems. Each thought the other was being officious and unco-operative. They later discovered that the leader of the church in the area had separately told each of them that he was in charge.

There is a delicate balance between allowing too much and too little freedom and responsibility. The position on the spectrum will vary according to the nature of the task and the experience of the person. In general, however, it is a good management principle to 'push decisions down the line.' Some leaders let themselves become cluttered with a mass of detail. John Adair quotes the company chairman who retained the decision on the size of paper clip to be used in the office.[3] Decision-making that is remote from the scene of action will tend to result in mistakes. A famous and extreme example is the charge of the Light Brigade. More mundane examples are church committees who take decisions about Sunday school materials without consulting the teachers, or office managers who order new photocopiers without consulting the secretaries that have to use them. Some leaders are afraid to delegate responsibility for fear of others' mistakes, but there can be no progress without experimentation and experimentation is bound to result in some errors. One innovative and successful company had as its eleventh commandment 'Make sure you generate a reasonable number of mistakes.' Theodore Roosevelt once said, 'The best executive is the one who has the sense enough to pick good men to do what he wants done and self-restraint enough not to keep meddling with them while they do it.'[4] Bishop David Sheppard of Liverpool, writing from his experience in East London, has said, 'The organised church must encourage spur of the moment "happenings". It must risk giving erratic leaders their head. . . .

This will mean that the church leadership is not able to keep control of events. Things may get out of hand. But that may allow the Holy Spirit to intervene.'[5]

Some tend to refer back too often and some too little. Embarrassment and conflict can be avoided if lines and boundaries of authority and responsibility are defined at the beginning. Does a retiring Sunday school teacher have the authority to approach someone else to take over or should he or she consult the Sunday school superintendent and the central leadership group first? Does the Sunday school superintendent have the authority to plan a new syllabus? Do the Young Wives have the freedom to plan a week-end away even if it clashes with the Harvest Festival? A useful compromise between too much freedom and too little is a request that there should be consultation before a final decision is made.

### Discuss the objectives

Wherever possible it is good to discuss goals and objectives when delegating; this will avoid a 'maintenance mentality'. Sunday school teachers might have the goal of increasing attendance by 10 per cent within a two-year period, or the objective of visiting the house of each child once a year. Some housegroups might have the goal of growing to the point of dividing and the objective of finding and training one or two assistant leaders. Goals need to be realistic and measurable, otherwise frustration will result; ideally they are discussed and agreed mutually, rather than being imposed from above.

### Arrange the training necessary

Too often volunteers are pitchforked into jobs without adequate preparation. Even reading lessons in church or leading the intercessions requires training, otherwise enthusiasm for 'every member ministry' can result in chaos. If the Youth Fellowship are planning a service and including

interviews they will need rehearsing in the use of a microphone. Some aspects of ministry, such as counselling, need
a regular and varied scheme of training. The principle of
shared leadership will mean that not all the teaching is done
by the professional minister. Key leaders should be released for specialist courses so that they can train others; on
other occasions a reading programme or cassette or video
course will be appropriate.

The ideal approach to training is a combination of
teaching and action. Not everyone will endorse every detail
of 'Evangelism Explosion'.[6] There are occasions when its
approach is too simplistic, but as a model of training it is
superb. The course lasts seventeen weeks and each evening
begins with a period of instruction; then each tutor takes
two trainees on a visit to homes in the area. At the end of
the evening there is a report back and discussion. At first
the trainees watch the tutor present the Gospel and then
they begin to present it themselves. After seventeen weeks
they may be invited to become tutors. Teaching divorced
from practice may result in volunteers always being under
instruction without becoming ready for service. The other
day I waited for thirty minutes at a bus stop before a bus
arrived. I was about to climb on board when I saw the
notice 'Not in service; driver under instruction'. Some
churches are like that bus – always planning training
programmes, but not always ready for service.

## Provide the support required

Most tasks need equipment and materials and therefore a
budget. Church committees are not always realistic in the
amounts they are prepared to set aside for teaching and
communication, yet they are ready to raise large sums to
repair the roof or the boiler. There is also the need for
human and spiritual resources. For some tasks it will be
valuable to arrange prayer partners and a support group.
For example, a team that is undertaking evangelistic visiting will need the support of others praying at home.

Sometimes a good deal of very basic and practical support is required. The minister in an inner city parish had difficulty in starting house groups because people were not used to opening their homes and in the beginning he ferried round extra cups and saucers and folding chairs.

## Plan a reporting system

This is the aspect of delegation that is most often neglected. Everyone who has a task of ministry needs a regular opportunity to discuss that task with an appropriate leader; in the case of a Sunday school teacher it may be the superintendent. This discussion may arise informally and spontaneously, but there is often value in a more structured, formal assessment. Every Christian has his or her strong points and weak points. We all need encouragement to develop the strong points and overcome the weak ones. In the South American Missionary Society we found that church leaders sometimes shied away from discussing the weak points of missionaries in their area until on occasion the problems escalated to the point of a breakdown in relationships. An early, open discussion would have given opportunity to work through the difficulties. The same difficulties can occur on staff teams in British churches. Christians can run away from conflict. A secretary ruefully exclaimed, 'It is easier working in a secular office; in a Christian organisation people are "too nice" and bury resentment rather than expressing it openly.' The result is an indefinable 'atmosphere' without opportunity to clear the air.

With the agreement of overseas church leaders we instituted a Job Assessment system. Once every twelve or eighteen months a missionary would complete a job assessment form and meet with his or her supervisor to discuss it. The supervisor would have completed an identical form prior to the meeting so that the different answers could be compared. The overall aim was one of positive encouragement and not negative criticism, and often the missionary discovered that he was undervaluing himself. The attitudes of the supervisor as well as those of the missionary were open for discussion. When we instituted the same system in our English office I found that my secretary's life was being made unnecessarily difficult by some of my working methods. Until the job assessment took place she had been too gracious to raise the issues. Some dioceses in the Church of England have instituted a system of job appraisals. In one case the description of the scheme is 'Joint Work Consultation' with the aim of developing 'ministry by objectives'. The consultation is primarily concerned with planning for the future rather than carrying out a post-mortem on the past, and it aims to plan objectives, talk them over, and then look at them again at the end of a time period. A vicar will consult with his Area Dean, the Area Dean with his Archdeacon and the Archdeacon with his Bishop. The hope is that as clergy find value in this kind of consultation they will plan similar ones with leaders in their parishes 'to give them the encouragement and the support they need'.

It is advisable that whatever system of reporting is used, whether formal or informal, written or verbal, frequent or infrequent, that it is established when an appointment is made. If it is introduced later it may be misunderstood as a sign of lack of confidence or mistrust. Similarly it is wise for some appointments to be made for a specific period – perhaps five years. This gives the possibility of review and change without crisis and conflict.

The following extract from a job assessment form is designed as an illustration rather than as a blueprint:

*Job role*
1. Has your job role been clearly defined?
2. What is it?
3. How far are you happy with it?

*Job performance*
1. What strengths have been revealed?
2. What weaknesses?

*Job guidance*
1. To what person(s) are you responsible?
2. Is the guidance you get too little, too much or just right?

*Job relationships with others*
1. Are these good, average or poor?
2. What can be done to improve them?

*Job development and training*
1. What do you see as the objectives and programme for the coming year?
2. Can you see any needed developments in your role, your job, or the work as a whole?
3. How far has the training you have received so far been adequate for your task?
4. Is there any further training you might need?

*Job support*
1. Are you receiving enough financial support? What are the needs for the next year?
2. Are you receiving enough support from others?

## Delegation leading to handover

In some cases the final step in the process of delegation is a complete handover. A missionary is expected to work himself out of a job in order to hand over to local, national leadership. This is part of Roland Allen's principle of creating self-supporting, self-propagating and self-governing churches.[7] Should the same principle apply in Britain? It could lead to a greater explosion of ministers and leaders. It could more quickly create a genuine local leadership in Urban Priority Areas and other districts if the middle-class 'missionary' imported from outside handed over after a period of time. His relationship to local leaders has in one sense to be that of John the Baptist to Jesus: 'He must become greater; I must become less' (John 3:30). Barnabas was remarkable not only for his ministry of encouragement, but also for his willingness to let Paul take the centre of the stage; the second fiddle is always the most difficult instrument to play. The change takes place in Acts

13; chapter 12:25 begins with the words 'When Barnabas and Saul had finished this mission', but chapter 13:13 begins 'From Paphos, Paul and his companions sailed to Perga'. Barnabas moves from the centre of the stage as Paul comes into the spotlight. Usually we are too slow to hand over. When Paul declared, 'From Jerusalem all the way around to Illyricum, I have fully proclaimed the gospel of Christ' (Romans 15:19), he had in fact simply established small cells in scattered households in strategic cities. However, these cells had been established in such a way as to be self-propagating.

Developing others' gifts and experience to the point when we can hand over to them is one of the key secrets of growth. The aim of one company executive was expressed in these words, 'Just as we have reserves for building, and equipment for future expansion, so we must have reserves of men trained to step into more responsible positions.'[8] It is easier to say than to practise. A missionary nurse described it this way: 'If you want a job well done, do it yourself; if you want it to last, get someone else to do it.'

A further dimension of delegation is not just to train others for ministry, but to train them as leaders who will be

Stage one:
    The leader and his trainees

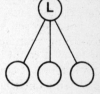

Stage two:
    The trainees become leaders training others

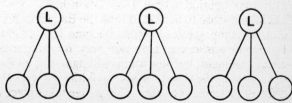

able to train others in turn. Paul instructed Timothy, 'The things you have heard me say . . . entrust to reliable men who will also be qualified to teach others' (2 Timothy 2:2). This is the explosion principle envisaged in the 'Evangelism Explosion' programme. Trainees become leaders who train others in turn. It is one thing to receive instruction but another to be able to communicate it to others; the real test of learning is the ability to communicate what has been learnt.

Tasks and programmes may be delegated to individuals, but they may also be delegated to teams. Very often this cannot be done without a review and change of structures; this will be the subject of the next chapter.

# 7 RENEWING THE STRUCTURES

## Managing a leadership explosion

Structures that free leadership

Different eldership schemes

Three 'levels' of structure

Matrix management

The 'super church' and the smaller church

There is a healthy suspicion of structures. The most perfect structures in the world will not by themselves lead to renewal, but on the other hand the wrong structures will hinder it. 'When we look back at the period since 1945, we see the renewal movement imprisoned in carefully defined and tentative experiments which were never allowed to become a strategy . . . When the world changed around us the churches remained the same.'[1] Structures either freeze us or free us. They are either like a scaffold that kills life or like scaffolding that provides a framework for effective leadership. The blessings of the Reformation were limited because there was a failure to change structures; the priest became a presbyter or pastor, but the professional divide from the laity still remained.

## Eldership schemes

Introducing shared leadership will nearly always lead to a change in structure. Of course it is traditional in the Church

of England for the vicar to share some aspects of leadership
with a Parochial Church Council just as in a Baptist church
the pastor will share with his deacons. When a new pastoral
leadership group or 'elders' scheme is set up, however,
there are bound to be questions. What will be the relationship between the 'elders' and the church-wardens,
the 'readers' and the PCC, or with the lay pastors, deacons
and church meeting? In some churches the 'elders' include
full-time staff, church-wardens and readers and are in
effect the standing committee of the PCC. The advantage of
this approach is that the elders are automatically integrated
into the traditional structures without radical change. The
disadvantage is that they have to deal with finance and
fabric as well as with pastoral issues and one of the main
reasons for their 'setting apart' is thereby lost. In other
cases the elders have not included all the full-time staff or
all the readers. There can be understandable resentment if
those who have undergone considerable periods of training
are not included in the elders' group, especially if some of
those in the group have had minimal training. In one parish
I visited the curate was not an elder. It is true that he was
relatively young and inexperienced, but he was bound to
wonder why he had spent five years at college. Similar
questions have been asked by readers who have undergone
extensive training during evenings and week-ends. On the
other hand not every reader has pastoral gifts and it may
defeat part of the object if the elders' group is dominated by
staff and readers. One church in the North of England has
resolved the problem by having all their elders trained and
officially licensed as readers. Another parish in the North
has set apart a group of Pastoral Leaders. One is responsible for oversight of pastoral, teaching and nurture groups,
another is responsible for oversight of youth and children's
work, another for witness and home and overseas mission,
and another for church services and family life. The assistant clergy are responsible for the teaching, training and
pastoral care of these Pastoral Leaders, while the church-
wardens and PCC are responsible for the administrative

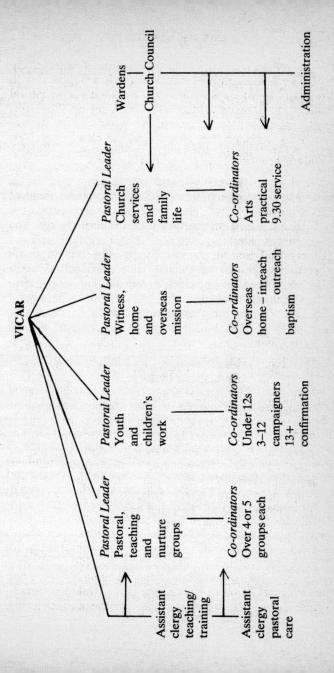

back up. An interesting feature is that while the parish has daughter churches the leadership of these churches is in the hands of 'lay' leaders and the function of the assistant clergy is to service them through teaching, training and pastoral support.

An Administry paper published in 1982[2] lists five types of elders' groups set up in Anglican churches –

1. Those composed of full-time staff.
2. Those based on traditional church structures, including, for example, staff, church-wardens and readers.
3. Those based on pastoral care structures – e.g. house group leaders.
4. Those based on the church council – the elders are a sub-committee of the church council or its standing committee. In one or two cases the eldership group is the church council.
5. Those where members are appointed simply on the basis of the gifts they display and not because of any office they hold.

Each type has its advantages and disadvantages and the choice will be influenced by local conditions, and by the philosophy behind the scheme. If we see elders primarily as having a pastoral role then the house group pattern may be the most appropriate. If their main role is teaching then the elders may be the staff and readers. If their role is one of overall management then they may be the standing committee of the church council. In many churches their role is a combined one of teaching and pastoral care. The method of appointment varies, too. In some cases the election is by the church council. In other cases the church council approves the scheme, but leaves the choice of individual to the vicar. Sometimes there is a commissioning by the bishop. Whatever the approach the powers, accountability and relationships of pastoral leaders or elders need to be clearly defined. Committees and groups as well as individuals need job descriptions. A vicar in the Midlands described his church council as having had an identity crisis after their eldership scheme had been set up and a church council in the South felt it had become a 'rubber stamp' for the elders' decisions. The right balance needs to be struck. As we have seen (p. 64) the Jerusalem conference in Acts 15 allowed for discussion and debate among the apostles and elders as well as with the whole church. Individual leaders – Peter, Barnabas, Paul and James – make significant contributions, but the final decision is recorded in these words: 'Then the apostles and elders, with the whole church . . .' (v 22). The elders give a lead, but they do so with the church, not on behalf of the church.

Similar questions about relationships between the new structures and the old are raised in Baptist churches. What is to be the relationship of the elders or pastoral leaders with the deacons and the church meeting? Paul Beasley Murray and Alan Wilkinson describe how the deacons in their church were not happy with the idea of an eldership scheme on the grounds that it would put an extra tier into the church management structure.[3] Instead they set up teams for pastoral care, social action, evangelism and nurturing. These teams are responsible to the deacons and through them to the church meeting. A Baptist church which has set up an elders' scheme is described on pages 102–3.

## Three 'levels' of structure

Churches themselves can be put into categories according to the size and complexity of their leadership structures. At *level one* everyone relates directly to the professional minister or leader. At *level two* there are a number of groups which relate to a central leadership group. Normally it is the group leader who is the representative on the central group, but it can be another member. The groups may be house groups or cells located in different geographical areas – on housing estates, in a private housing development, perhaps in a factory. They may be functional groups, specialising in youth work, evangelism, worship or communication. They may be a mixture of geographical and functional groups.

Once a church grows beyond a certain point it is difficult for everyone to relate directly to one professional leader on a day-to-day basis. In industry the maximum 'span of control' is normally between seven and twelve. David Wasdell has shown that once a church gets beyond 150 in size there seems to be a ceiling on further growth; this is mainly because it is difficult for individuals to know one another and have a sense of belonging beyond that size. The answer is to move from a level one structure to a level two or three.

At *level three* there are sector or area leadership groups (S) which are each related to the central leadership group (C). This stage is often necessary in large and complex churches, though the principle can be relevant in smaller churches, too. A sector leadership group, for example, could be composed of all the housegroup leaders in a particular area, or it could be composed of the leaders of different children's organisations.

One large Baptist church which has a level three structure divided up their district into five geographical areas.

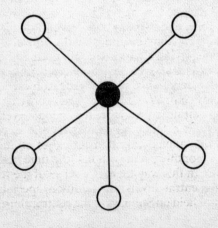

Level one

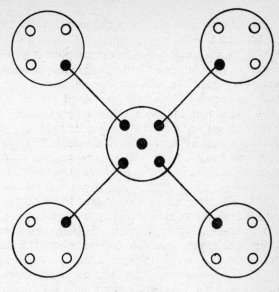

Level two

Each area has ten or more house groups under the oversight of two elders. In the Gospels Jesus frequently sent out disciples in pairs, and it has been found in this Baptist eldership scheme that pairing provides an essential mutual support. Only one of the two, however, attends the central elders' meeting, thus ensuring that the central meeting does not become too large. Once a month the members of all ten house groups in an area have a joint meeting organised by their two elders. This gives a geographical identity and wider fellowship. While house groups provide the opportunity of getting to know a few people well, the area meeting gives a fuller range of gifts and experience. In addition the 'annual church meeting' of all members has become a monthly event with half the time being set aside for prayer. In this way there is a sense of identity at local, area and central levels. In addition specialist training sessions are held on Sundays in the central church building.

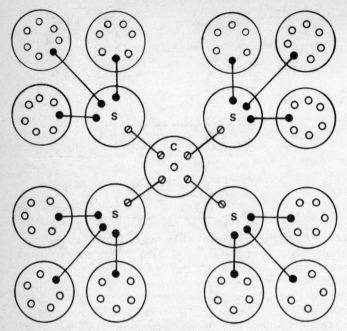

Level three

Similarly a large Anglican church has divided its membership into four large 'care groups'. Each care group is divided in turn into eight or ten discipleship groups. It was found that discipleship groups on their own did not give enough scope for the full range of gifts or for wider sharing. In addition there are ministry groups which specialise, for example, in the care of the elderly, in counselling, social involvement, drama and music. Church members are expected to belong to all three types of group, having both a 'vertical' and a 'horizontal' commitment.

Care groups and ministry groups meet once a month; discipleship groups meet once a fortnight. In smaller churches the 'care group' would simply be a monthly central meeting for all members. These ministry teams are

CARE GROUPS

| | | 1 | 2 | 3 | 4 |
|---|---|---|---|---|---|
| **MINISTRY** | Intercession | | | | |
| | Evangelism | | | | |
| **TEAMS** | Counselling | | | | |
| | Music/Drama | | | | |
| | Etc | | | | |

an interesting dimension and they suggest that the diagrams above are too simplistic (pp. 102–4). There may or may not be the full range of pastoral, counselling, teaching and evangelistic gifts in each house group but even if there are, those with specific gifts are often strengthened as they meet others who have similar gifts. For example, it is ideal if two or three members of a house group are prepared to visit homes in their area, but they may need the support and experience of a central, specialist visiting team.

## Avoiding the bottleneck

Advocates of leadership groups or of elders' schemes sometimes base their arguments on the danger of a professional minister becoming a bottleneck. However, the elders can also become a bottleneck. The same is true of the central group in levels two and three on pages 103–4 and of the sector leadership groups at level three. It may make no difference in the diagrams overleaf whether the circle marked 'L' is an individual leader or a group. Furthermore a group may only meet fortnightly or monthly and become an even greater delaying factor than one-man or staff

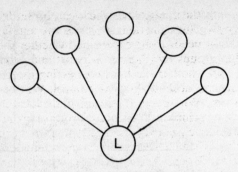

**A tightly controlled structure**

leadership. The answer is to establish lines of relationship that do not have to go through the centre. A tightly controlled committee meeting is one where all discussion goes through the chairman. A loosely controlled house-group is one where the leader stimulates interaction between all members.

The same principle applies to groups. If the Sunday school wants to discuss its finances it may be better for it to do so direct with the Finance and Fabric committee rather than through the central leadership group. Ideally the job description for each group will determine which issues have

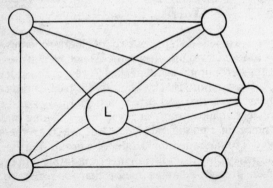

**A loosely controlled structure**

to come into the centre and which can be settled direct. While the structure diagrams for levels two and three have their value it needs to be established whether the central leadership groups are there to support and service or to manage and whether the lines connecting the circles are lines of advice, accountability or control. We need to face the question, 'Where is the basic unit of the local church? Is it to be found primarily in the house group or in the centre?'

Some mission agencies are developing what is known as the 'matrix' system of leadership. For example, an agency working in Africa, Asia and Latin America may have departments for each of these areas as well as separate departments for finance, personnel and publicity. How do these departments relate? If all decisions have to go through a central board or even a central staff meeting there will again be a bottleneck.

The matrix approach is to have regular meetings along both vertical and horizontal lines. Within the Finance department, for example, there will be one or more who have special responsibility for Africa and who will attend the Africa department meeting, while other members of the Finance department will attend the Asia or Latin America department meetings. On the other hand there will be some in the Africa department who attend Finance,

| Functional Departments | | Regional Departments | |
|---|---|---|---|
| | Africa | Asia | Latin America |
| Finance | | | |
| Personnel | | | |
| Publicity | | | |

some Personnel and some Publicity meetings. One of the advantages of this method is that emergency discussions can be held as needed. If the emergency concerns a financial need in Africa, a quick meeting would be set up at the intersection of 'Finance' and 'Africa' involving the appropriate representatives from those departments. Similarly if the issue is the relocation of a worker in Asia the meeting would include representatives from 'Personnel' and 'Asia'. Of course regular board meetings are still needed as well in order to decide general policy and to monitor the functioning of the departments.

There are, however, some disadvantages. It can be confusing, especially in the early stages, while staff can feel that they have two bosses and therefore be unsure which should have the priority. One answer is to determine that either the vertical or the horizontal lines should have priority; in the diagrams below and on page 109 the priority lies with the unbroken vertical lines.

If a matrix chart were drawn for a local church it might look something like this. Local churches depend on volunteers and not just on full-time staff and so it would be unwise and impossible to have the numbers of meetings that offices using this system can. However, it is a useful illustration to help us see how lines of relationship can be

| Functions | Geographical Areas | | | |
|---|---|---|---|---|
| | North | East | South | West |
| Youth Work | | | | |
| Evangelism | | | | |
| Publicity, etc. | | | | |

varied. All too often it is assumed that the complex structures of church life can be reduced to one diagram and that the lines of relationship are of only one kind. The level three structure illustrated on page 104 could put an impossible pressure on the central leadership unless a matrix approach is used or unless the majority of decisions are taken in the sector leadership groups. Delegation of decision-making is best illustrated below by making the sector groups functional. For the sake of clarity only a few sector groups are shown, and only some of the lines of relationship. The central group has a monitoring function rather than a controlling one and this is therefore a systemic or organic model rather than a classical or bureaucratic one (see pp. 25–7).

A distinction is sometimes drawn between 'line management' and 'consultant management'; the former has day-to-day responsibility for leadership and the latter is responsible for training and for agreeing goals and objectives. In

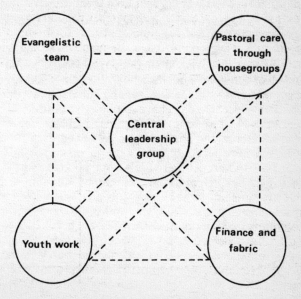

the daughter churches described on pages 98–9 the lay leadership would be line management and the assistant clergy be consultant management.

## The 'super church' and the smaller church

All this no doubt seems very remote and even laughable to the average church which is small enough for first- or second-level leadership structures. However, it is often useful for such churches to establish links with other smaller churches or with a larger church in the same area. In this way a wider range of ministry and training can be provided. At one point we were in a smaller church in West London and in touch with a group of twenty teenagers who were mainlining on heroin. Ten of them eventually died from overdoses or from polluted supplies. Ministry to this group was costly in terms of time and patience and we were grateful for the help of a young Christian couple. Eventually this couple moved away and we were desperately looking for a replacement. One day I found myself standing by the coffin of one of the addicts whose body had been brought home for twenty-four hours before the funeral. The next day as I went door-to-door visiting I found a houseful of Christian students who lived in the same street but commuted to fashionable 'super' churches a few miles away. Ever since that day I have wondered if more could be done by way of sharing training and ministry between 'super' churches and smaller ones. We need each other. Otherwise the super churches become 'talent mountains' or 'gift lakes'. In fairness there are several good examples of larger churches helping smaller ones and sometimes the latter are resistant to help from outside. Leaders of both super and smaller churches need to keep looking beyond their immediate boundaries. The ideal might be a satellite relationship where the 'super church' provides training, support and specialist skills and the smaller church provides an outlet for exercising ministry. There are, of course, dangers. Those in the 'super church' might be of a different social background or culture from those in the smaller church and might be tempted to think they had everything to give and nothing to receive. These are dangers to be overcome particularly in overseas missionary work. The first step is to open lines of communication, especially when there are 'super church' members living in smaller church areas.

A fascinating illustration of leadership structures that stretch more widely than the local church is the Ichthus Fellowship in South East London. Ichthus describes itself as a church, a Bible school and a missionary society. Its aim is to plant between sixty and eighty congregations in a ten-year period. Young people come for a year's experience of church planting and urban mission, but many stay longer. Instead of placing an isolated missioner into a new area a group of Christians are transplanted and become an embryo church. The Gospel can then be shared by demonstration as well as by proclamation. They begin by meeting in a house and then as numbers grow they move into a school or into an empty church building. One of the secrets is the mobility and flexibility of the leadership. The best ministry and leadership available goes into the smallest congregations until they are established and growing. These smaller congregations are encouraged by a pattern of Sunday worship which combines local services with a large central 'celebration' where all congregations come together.

Ichthus, of course, has the advantages – and the dangers – of a para-church organisation which is not fettered by denominational structures. However, mainline denominations already have structures which are wider than the local church and there are examples of congregations who transplant a group of their members into a new area. There are several examples where members from a lively church have deliberately moved house into a neighbouring area where the church is moribund or has been made redundant. As a result the moribund church has taken a new lease of life.

## Committees or groups

In the leadership structures described in this chapter the component parts have been described as groups. This is a deliberate use of a neutral word. Some groups will be committees, but others will be task or action groups, teams or coalitions. Sometimes an elder or other individual will be given responsibility together with the freedom to form a support group as necessary. The word 'committee' to some ears implies talk rather than action. Committees have been described as 'cul-de-sacs' into which good ideas are lured and quietly strangled. They can stifle creativity and blunt decision-making. It is wise for there to be at least one main committee, democratically elected, with regular meetings and minutes which are open to scrutiny by all church members. This ensures that the central leadership group does not become or does not appear to be autocratic. On the other hand it is unwise to proliferate sub-committees. The proposal to set one up may betray an unwillingness to grasp the nettle of making a decision. Some will be necessary, but others will be more effective as action groups or teams which are responsible for carrying out and not just deciding strategy. There is also value in 'coalitions'. These are temporary groups set up for a particular purpose, such as a mission, and drawing on more permanent groups for its membership. Leaders continually need to ask what is the most appropriate structure for each task and to keep such structures under review. Yet change must not take place so frequently or quickly that church members become disorientated. In AD 60 Petronius Arbiter warned, 'We tend to meet every new situation by reorganising; and a wonderful method it can be for creating an illusion of progress while producing confusion, inefficiency and demoralisation.'[4]

There are other warnings that need to be heeded in looking at structures. The church is an organism, not an organisation, and relationships matter more than programmes. As one minister in the North of England put it, 'The Spirit blows where he wills; his solutions are rarely tidy.'

# 8   TURNED OUTWARD TO THE WORLD

God's plan embraces all creation

The relation of social action and evangelism

Community involvement

Structures for social action

Leadership in society

A global dimension

## God's plan for the world

Discussion so far has mainly centred on internal structures
and activities, on house groups, Sunday schools and finance
committees. But what of the church's mission in and to the
world? Canon Douglas Webster has said, 'Basically ministry is the church turned outward to the world, rather than
its internal organisation.'[1] On pages 50–1 we looked at
the pattern of leadership in Ephesians 4:11 (rsv): 'His gifts
were that some should be apostles, some prophets, some
evangelists, some pastors and teachers.' But Ephesians
4:11 must be seen in its context and the context is a
staggering global and cosmic plan 'to unite all things in him
(Christ), things in heaven and things on earth' (Ephesians
1:10 rsv). This unity is to transcend every division of race,
nationality, class and sex and within the overall plan the

church is to be God's model or pilot project of such unity (3:9–10). Individuals are redeemed and reconciled to God through Christ, but while 'the redemption of persons is the centre of God's plan . . . it is not the circumference of that plan'.[2] God's purposes for the world are not confined to the church.

## God's objectives for leaders

God's cosmic plan has radical implications for styles of leadership. The Christian leader must focus not only on the Lord and his church, but also on the Lord and his world. Sometimes we operate as if the Lord is active only in the church. We speak of 'bringing' Christ to the nations or to the local community, but in one sense Christ is there already, as 'the true light that gives light to every man' (John 1:9).

This is not to deny the presence of evil in a fallen world, or to suggest that the Christian leader endorses all that is said and done in society, but it does mean that he ought to be ready to look, listen and learn from the world around. God's cosmic plan also has the implication that the objectives of Christian leadership are not simply to fill pews.

What are the objectives? The debate tends to polarise between those who emphasise church growth and those who emphasise social action. The former quote Jesus' words in Matthew 28:19–20: 'Therefore go and make disciples of all nations, baptising them . . . teaching them to obey everything I have commanded you.' The latter quote Christ's sermon at Nazareth – 'The Spirit of the Lord is on me, because he has anointed me to preach good news to the poor. He has sent me to proclaim freedom for the prisoners and recovery of sight for the blind, to release the oppressed, to proclaim the year of the Lord's favour' (Luke 4:18–19).

But in Luke 4 the poor and the blind include those who suffer from spiritual poverty and blindness, while in

Matthew 28 the commands must include the one to love our neighbour. The passages need not be in opposition and both evangelism and social action are essential objectives. The measure of success in a Christian leadership group is therefore not only the numbers in church, it is also the health of the community around. 'The final test of a congregation's effectiveness lies not in how many people enter, but in what they take with them as they go back into society.'[3] As David Watson put it – 'When an individual responds to the gospel, he commits himself both to Christ and to the new society that Christ has come to build.'[4]

## Social action and evangelism

The relationship of the two objectives is a complex one. Evangelism can be a bridge to social action and vice versa, but ideally they go together. Social programmes should never consciously or unconsciously become an inducement to respond to the Gospel, but they can often be an effective witness to a God who cares. A missionary who had been instrumental in setting up shanty town workshops for the unemployed said, 'We demonstrate that we have a caring and a sharing God.'[5] Openness to the world will affect the Christian leader's understanding of his message and his mission. He will begin to see social concern as an important partner to evangelism and even a dimension of it. John the Baptist's challenge to the soldiers, the tax-collectors and those with full wardrobes (Luke 3:7–14) implied that repentance should have a social dimension. The pattern of Christian discipleship taught to new converts must include a socio-political involvement. Jim Wallis has said, 'Conversion is the beginning of active solidarity with the purposes of the kingdom of God . . . we are converted to compassion, justice and peace as we take our stand as citizens of Christ's new order . . . it is more than a promise of all that might be; it is also a threat to all that is.'[6]

## Trapped in the temple

So often our church traditions and structures make it difficult for the professional minister to be turned outward to the world. Howard Snyder argues that the Old Testament concepts of sacrifice, priesthood and temple have all been fulfilled in Christ – he is the sacrifice and the High Priest and the temple is wherever he is present among his people. Unfortunately the Reformation altered only the concepts of sacrifice and priesthood; the medieval priest became the Reformation pastor but his ministry still centred round a temple building.[7] Although the early church began by worshipping at the Jerusalem temple persecution soon drove them from it and finally it was destroyed in AD 70. The focus of their fellowship was in the homes of members. It has to be remembered, too, that in New Testament times the household was the basic social unit and therefore there was not the modern separation between church and society; the world of work, of family and of church coincided. There is, of course, a practical value in a building large enough to house the whole local church, but all too easily it sucks in our resources and dominates our thinking. In a London parish the leadership team were planning a mission strategy for a part of their area that had a 'mission' church building. Instead of asking 'what is the right strategy for this area?' and then deciding whether the mission church had a place in the strategy they were unconsciously asking the question 'how can we use our building more effectively?' As a result their organisations were 'come' structures rather than 'go' structures. There are parallels with the mission compound of Victorian missionary strategy; it has been well said that the mission station can all too easily become a stationary mission and then finish up as a mass of stationery.

Professional ministers are trained primarily for ministry in a 'temple'. Our thinking, teaching and programmes become temple orientated rather than world orientated and whatever the scripture text used in the sermon the application becomes an exhortation to support the temple events chronicled in the weekly notice sheet. A clergyman called on a leading executive in a multinational company who was faced with a moral dilemma: should he take a certain course of action which might result in 6,000 people in India losing their jobs? 'Have you talked this over with your local vicar?' asked the clergyman. 'Oh, no. Whenever he calls he asks to see the wife about the Women's Fellowship programme.' The clergyman later moved to the stockbroker belt and started a discussion group for business executives in order to help them relate their faith to the world of work. It is, of course, hard for the Christian leader who is expected to spend most of his time around the temple. The bigger and more complex the church the more this is likely to happen. Shared leadership which links those whose main work is in the world with those whose main work is in the temple should redress the balance and give opportunity to develop an awareness of needs in society and the Christian response to them. But this does not happen automatically. Agendas tend to be dominated and priorities shaped by temple needs, lay leaders become clericalised and their ministry seen mainly as temple ministry. It is not unusual to find leaders in the world of work harnessed to give out hymn books and take the collection; they end up living compartmentalised lives.

## Who writes the agenda?

A deliberate policy has to be established to tackle concerns outside the temple as well as inside. Shared leadership properly developed can give the opportunity to shape the teaching programme of the church so that it is turned outward to the world. According to the topic, sermon planning can begin with a discussion that includes union members, social workers or nurses and doctors. Some sermons can be a group production, or be replaced by a discussion or debate. A similar pattern can be established for planning the house group and adult teaching programme. There are, of course, two opposite dangers. One is that of being so pietistic or other-worldly that the teaching programme seems to have little relevance to daily life, but the other danger lies with those who say 'Let the world write the agenda.' It is good to let the world raise questions for the Christian faith to answer, provided that we do not forget that God has some questions to ask of the world.

There are opposite dangers, too, in making social and political pronouncements. It is fatally easy to make slick, superficial comments that are regretted at leisure. Frank Buchman, the originator of the Oxford Group or Moral Rearmament movement, declared on his return to New York after a visit to Germany, 'I thank God for a man like Adolf Hitler who built a front line of defence against the anti-christ of Communism.'[8]

Yet there is also the danger of silence. 'We will have to repent in this generation,' said Martin Luther King, 'not for the hateful actions of bad people, but for the appalling silence of the good.' Fife and Glasser criticise some early missionary leaders in China: 'They trained men as they themselves had been trained, with limited Christian perspective on the local church's place in society . . . great tribal churches were led by men who were abysmally indifferent to the corruption around them – opium traffic, feudal slavery, rapacious landlords, social injustice – and this in areas where the church represented a significant and sizeable segment in total society. . . .'[9]

## Community involvement

It may be easier for Christian leaders to be turned outward to the world when they are directly confronted with social need. The Christian life has a different perspective and different priorities in an Urban Priority Area or in an area of conflict than it does in suburbia. I was deeply impressed on a visit to South Africa to meet a Christian leader undertaking a public fast in order to help end the system of compulsory conscription into the armed services. Among South African whites there were a number, both Christian and non-Christian, who rebelled against a system that brought them into confrontation with their black brethren in the townships. This same leader had also joined others in silent protest against police action in one of the townships. He came from a background where socio-political involvement was the exception rather than the rule, but he had allowed his attitudes to be shaped by the context. Others, of course, had cut themselves off and taken refuge in a busy round of traditional temple activities. The leader concerned found his stance a costly one; many in his congregation, perhaps the majority, were either critical or puzzled at his action.

What can the leader do if he is not living in an area of obvious social need? He can be linked with such an area through study, visits, reading and correspondence. Places of acute deprivation can present in a stark way the problems that lie below the surface in many other areas. Some of the economic factors behind the global North/South divide have parallels in the South/North divide within Britain. The problems faced by many of the black population in Britain have been rightly described as 'the barium meal of society' and the focus on Urban Priority Areas has helped make ministers aware of needy areas in their own district. In our present parish there is an unofficial meeting of social workers, health visitors, police and church staff held once a quarter in the church lounge. It helps the church to become aware of the needs of the local community and it is the only forum where those who work in the community meet together. The church can thus provide a valuable bridge between professional and voluntary leaders and between one professional and another. With curtailment of social services and increasing need the hard-pressed professionals value the partnership of voluntary workers, while the latter benefit from specialist advice and guidance; there is nothing worse than 'do gooders' who think they know all the answers. A project team has resulted in order to research local needs prior to the setting up of a church counselling centre. There are occasions when both the professionals and the church workers need specialist advice; at one of our meetings, for example, we welcomed an expert on the needs of the elderly within the local Asian community.

## Structures for social action

For some needs it will be right to set up new organisations or structures, whether secular, Christian or mixed. Soon after I arrived in an Urban Priority Area a lady knocked at the door to ask for help. I mentally reached for a tract, but her problem was that she had been given an eviction notice by her landlord. Discussion with her, and with the landlord, led to a deeper appreciation of local housing problems and the setting up of a church housing association.

Counselling is another area where new structures for leadership may be needed. Church members will find themselves in contact with people who have psychiatric, marital or social problems that are beyond their experience or training. It is valuable to have a group of Christian leaders who have legal, medical or social work expertise and who are prepared to equip others in basic counselling. Such a group will not readily be available in many local churches, but it could be set up for a wider area.

There are other occasions when it is not right for the church to set up structures of its own, but for the Christian leader to join secular organisations. There are valid arguments for Christian youth clubs and church schools, but it is also important to have Christian leaders acting as salt in secular ones. The leader working in a secular organisation must avoid giving the impression that he has all the answers, but there will be times when he can bring Christian insights to bear; he can, for instance, be more detached than others are from the pressure of political party lines.

Some years ago I had the privilege of chairing an adventure playground committee set up by local politicians from the two major parties in order to help deprived children. The church is not the only body to fall victim to dogma and in this instance national political policies were being applied inappropriately to the local scene. There was pressure to run the playground entirely from the Town Hall, with paid professional staff; instead the committee were persuaded to harness and develop the gifts in the local community by using a mixed team of professionals and volunteers – working 'with' people, rather than 'for' them. Similarly the Christian leader can have a valuable ministry as a school governor, whether he or she is a party or a 'non-political' appointee.

One of the difficulties for a Christian professional working in a secular organisation is that it is considered 'unprofessional' to mention faith in a counselling context. Some take this to extremes and miss the opportunity for sharing faith even where the 'client' seems to be seeking it. However, the difficulty underlines the need to have Christian leaders working within Christian organisations as well as within secular ones. An overtly Christian medical practice will be able to provide holistic counselling for spiritual as well as mental and physical needs. Social services provide for immediate specific needs, but the church at its best can provide a caring community and extended family where the hurts of the past can be healed and the individual given the love, support and sense of worth that enables him to develop into a whole person. This is vitally important in Urban Priority Areas where the breakdown of family life is as big a factor as deprivation in housing and education.

Frequently a Christian fellowship group is set up within a school, a factory or an office. Some see these cells rather than the traditional congregation as being the strategic church of the future.[10] Valuable as they are their importance is limited, especially in a day of rising unemployment.

Roger Greenway has said,

A few years ago writers were saying that in the urban, industrialised environment primary groups, such as the family, were of less importance, and secondary groups, composed of one's fellow workers outside the home, were the most meaningful to the individual urbanite. This was one of the premises on which the industrial mission approach was built . . . today this is no longer assumed . . . the family is still very important in meeting the needs of urban people. In the home certain needs are met – companionship, affection, basic security – which can be met nowhere else. Urban man's most basic identity still is connected with his home.[11]

## Leadership in society

It is important that we define Christian leadership in terms of those who take a lead in society and not just in terms of leadership in the temple. Many church vestries have a map of their district with flags pinned at appropriate points to show where members' homes are located, but there ought to be a second set of flags to show where members work. Mission strategy must centre on both kinds of flag. A curate confessed, 'We were working out how to "get into" the local hospital when we suddenly realised that we already had several members working there.' Such people need identifying and they may need a special support group and appropriate training to help them bring Christian perspectives to bear on the problems they face. The congregation need to be aware of their needs so that they can support them in prayer. Sunday intercessions tend to polarise between international and national crises on the one hand and on the sick and bereaved within the congregation on the other and very often the local community is left out. One Baptist church has encouraged Christian leaders in strategic jobs to share their needs through regular newsletters that are then circulated to the congregation.

The danger of the structure diagrams in Chapter 7 is that

they are temple orientated. A church leadership that is 'turned outwards' to the world might produce a diagram like the one below. So often a mission map needs to be made up of dynamic arrows, not static symbols. Whatever the structure it is vital that the Christian leader in society is not fettered by being expected to attend church activities night after night. It would be good to carry out a 'mission audit' to find out the balance in leaders' diaries – how much time is spent on temple meetings, how much time with the family, and how much with non-Christian friends and neighbours.

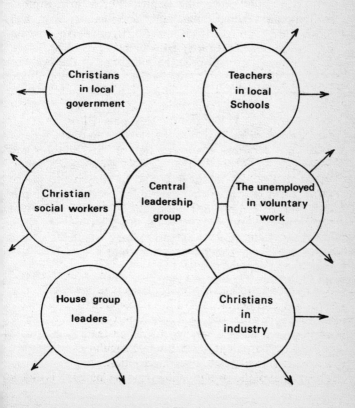

## A global dimension

The leader needs to be open not only to the immediate
world around, but also to the world at large. Contact with
Christians in other lands can be refreshing and stimulating.
On a visit to Chile I attended a Pentecostal cathedral where
there were 500 in the choir and a total membership of
80,000. The congregation were divided into four and each
quarter came to the central church once a month, while on
other Sundays they worshipped in their own locality. I had
come from an area in London where the Methodist church
had been pulled down, the Baptist church turned into a
second-hand furniture mart and the Salvation Army hall
destroyed by vandals. It gave me a different perspective on
the possibilities of church growth in deprived areas. In
1 Corinthians 12 Paul uses the metaphor of the body to
illustrate our mutual interdependence and responsibility
for one another. 'The eye cannot say to the hand, "I don't
need you!" And the head cannot say to the feet, "I don't
need you!"' (v 21) Nor can the European Christian say to
the African, or the Asian to the North American, 'I don't
need you!' God has given us different gifts, cultures and
styles of church life so that we can enrich each other.
It would be false to suggest that all church life in the
third world is rosy or that everything on our doorstep is
dull, but we can be enriched by the joy and creativity of
Christians from other lands. We shall see in Chapter 12 how
theological education by extension, for example, has much
to teach us about training for leadership.

# 9 SERVANT LEADERSHIP

Jesus' servant model as a challenge to authoritarian leadership

Identification as the secret of openness and trust

The leader's example and weaknesses

The use and abuse of authority – the house church movement

The source of authority

Suffering

## The challenge to authoritarian leadership

In Chapter 2 we looked at different styles of leadership around the world – a strong charismatic style among Latin American Pentecostals, a feudal one in Asia, a tribal style in Africa and a strong executive one in the United States. It is important to appreciate the style that is considered normal in each society and therefore what will be expected in each local church. But we are called to judge society and its culture by the standards of the Gospel and in Mark 10 Jesus contrasts his servant style of leadership with the authoritarian one common in the world of his day – 'You know that those who are regarded as rulers of the Gentiles lord it over them, and their high officials exercise authority over them. Not so with you. Instead, whoever wants to become great among you must be your servant, and whoever wants to be first must be slave of all. For even the Son of Man did not come to be served, but to serve, and to give his life as a ransom for many' (vv 42–5). Similarly Peter exhorts his fellow leaders – 'Be shepherds of God's flock . . . not lording it over those entrusted to you, but being examples to the flock' (1 Peter 5:2–3).

The servant model is not altogether popular today. People admire strong leaders even if they disagree with their policies. Prime Minister Margaret Thatcher found her popularity soaring as she took a strong lead at the time of the South Atlantic war and the desire for certainty and strong leadership has made possible an increase of fundamentalism in world religions. Sometimes this desire is linked with irresponsibility and laziness – we want someone else to think through the problems and come up with the answers and then we can blame them and not ourselves if things go wrong.

## Identification

What does it mean in practice to be a 'servant' leader? The first principle is one of identification. In order to identify with those he came to save Christ was willing to be stripped of privilege, position and power. Paul says, 'Your attitude should be the same as that of Christ Jesus: Who, being in very nature God, did not consider equality with God something to be grasped, but made himself nothing, taking the very nature of a servant, being made in human likeness. And being found in appearance as a man, he humbled himself and became obedient to death – even death on a cross!' (Philippians 2:5–8)

Although we have referred to the Latin American Pentecostal pastor as an example of strong charismatic leadership (p. 31) the other side of the picture is that church members are able to identify with their pastor as 'one of us'. This is the secret of his success: 'He who preaches is brother to him who listens; they belong to the same social class and share the weight of the same problems of making a living.'[1]

Identification leads to openness, friendship and trust, as a missionary agriculturist found after spending five hours of the night in thigh-deep mud in order to recover a truck from a hole. 'This kind of experience proves the value of working with people and not just directing them. Now the old converted witch doctor takes me by the hand like a son.' A church-warden in an inner city parish said in admiration of his vicar, 'You can often see him hard at work, clearing out the church drains.' It might have been wiser to set up and join a working party but by coming out of the study and rolling up his sleeves that vicar had bridged the gap between a bookish and non-bookish culture. While his work was primarily that of 'the ministry of the word and prayer' the occasional 'serving at tables' did wonders for identification.

Identification includes being seen on the front line. Montgomery complained of an earlier generation of generals who never left their comfortable headquarters to tell their subalterns and men what was going to happen.[2] In Ho Chi Minh's army generals and colonels were to be found alongside privates, and this was seen to be the secret of their twenty-five year survival and ultimate victory in Vietnam. 'There is nothing to distinguish their generals from their private soldiers except the star they wear on their collars . . . their colonels go on foot like privates. They live on the rice they carry on them, or the tubers they pull out of the forest earth, on the fish they catch. . . . No pre-packaged rations, no cars or fluttering pennants . . . no military bands. But victory!'[3] It might be argued that top leaders are too busy running the organisation to be involved at the grassroots, but the leader of a large church who spends all his time at the top of the pyramid will quickly become out of touch. In industry successful managers are those who spend time on the shop floor.[4] It was encouraging to meet a third world bishop who regularly engaged in door-to-door visiting with members of his local church.

The principle of identification can be as costly for ministers living in inner city areas as it is for missionaries going overseas. In one parish the church-wardens asked a prospective vicar 'Will you be sending your children to the local school?' His predecessor had distanced himself and his family by using private education. The difficulty of this decision must not be minimalised, however; in some cases the minister's children find it difficult to adapt, can become withdrawn or even traumatised and because of their father's job may suffer negative discrimination. Yet if they are sufficiently resilient and have good family support they can receive a depth of experience and an ability to relate to a wide cross-section of people. By living in the area the minister may be the only resident professional as very often teachers, doctors and social workers commute in. Yet the report of the Archbishop's Commission on Urban Priority Areas showed that job satisfaction can be high in such areas.[5]

Servant leaders are those who are ready to get close to people. A few generations ago ministers were warned not to have close friends for fear of forming a clique. Cliques must, of course, be avoided and ministers must be available to all, but it is unnatural not to have close friendships. We have seen how Jesus spent time with the crowds, but also drew apart to be with the twelve and sometimes just with the three who were closest to him. Sometimes we are slow to form friendships for fear of rejection or of being let down, but this is part of the risk as Jesus found with Peter and even more with Judas. An effective youth leader was once described as someone with 'an infinite capacity for being let down'.

## Shepherds and stewards

One of the favourite Bible words used to describe the Christian leader is the word 'shepherd'. The shepherd shares life with his flock out in the fields, exposed to all weathers and facing danger from wolf and robber. He epitomises the idea of service. In Ezekiel 34 the Lord describes himself as the model shepherd; 'I myself will search for my sheep . . . I will rescue them . . . and I will bring them into their own land. I will pasture them' (vv 11–13). 'I will search for the lost and bring back the strays. I will bind up the injured' (v 16). In John's Gospel, chapter 10, Jesus describes himself as the Good Shepherd in contrast both to the thief who exploits and to the hired worker who is simply concerned for his wage packet. The ministry of seeking, healing and watching over others is the essence of servant leadership.

Another common word used to describe servant leadership is 'steward'. Paul says, 'This is how one should regard us, as servants [literally 'under-rowers'] of Christ and stewards of the mysteries of God' (1 Corinthians 4:1 RSV). The steward was responsible for supplying food and other necessities to the slaves in a large household so that they could do their work effectively; when they came in from the fields he would have a meal ready for them. His service equipped them for service. But he was usually a slave himself, not owning the resources, but having to account for them to the master. The resources made available to the minister by the master include the grace and power of the Holy Spirit and the word of God. The ministry or service of the word is a dominant theme in the New Testament. The apostles arrange to have others appointed to distribute food to widows so that they can devote themselves to prayer and 'the ministry of the word' (Acts 6:1–4). Timothy is to be equipped for his ministry with the scriptures: 'All scripture is God-breathed and is useful for teaching, rebuking, correcting and training in righteousness, so that the man of God may be thoroughly equipped for every good work' (2 Timothy 3:16–17). He is to 'preach the word' at every opportunity (4:2) and is to become skilled at correctly handling it (2 Timothy 2:15).

## Example

The servant leader must be ready to lead by example and not just by exhortation. He must be a playing captain and not just a coach who shouts from the touchline, or the pulpit. We have seen this already in 1 Peter 5:3 (p. 126). Paul could say in his farewell address to the leaders of the church at Ephesus, 'You know how I lived the whole time I was with you . . . I have not coveted anyone's silver or gold or clothing . . . these hands of mine supplied my own needs and the needs of my companions. In everything I did, I showed you that by this kind of hard work we must help the weak' (Acts 20:18, 33–5). He told Timothy, 'Set an example for the believers in speech, in life, in love, in faith and in purity' (1 Timothy 4:12). The leader is to set an example by his temperance and self-control, by his readiness to give hospitality and by his ability to manage his family well (1 Timothy 3:4). The leader who exhorts without setting an example lets his life undermine his teaching. Jesus had to warn his followers about the Pharisees: 'The teachers of the law and the Pharisees sit in Moses' seat. So you must obey them and do everything they tell you. But do not do what they do, for they do not practise what they preach' (Matthew 23:2–3). Francis Bacon said, 'He that gives good advice builds with one hand. He that gives good counsel and example builds with both. But he that gives good admonition and bad example builds with one hand and pulls down with the other.'[6]

## The leader's weaknesses

The danger of a book on leadership and this chapter in particular is that it may set unrealistic standards. We must remember that even great leaders, such as Moses, David and Simon Peter, experienced major weaknesses and failures. It sometimes seems that great leaders make great mistakes. The minister should try to lead by example, but this does not mean a hypocritical pretence at perfection.

Even if we do not admit our mistakes and failures others will recognise them. John Adair gives this enchanting list:

*A Short Course on Leadership*

The six most important words:
'I admit I made a mistake.'
The five most important words:
'I am proud of you.'
The four most important words:
'What is your opinion?'
The three most important words:
'If you please.'
The two most important words:
'Thank you.'
The one most important word:
'We.'
And the least most important word:
'I.'[7]

A leader who is ready to admit mistakes and failure may have a much wider ministry than one who always appears highly organised and self-sufficient. Others will be ready to come and talk through their problems with someone who also suffers from weakness, provided that he knows some answers to that weakness. Although Jesus did not make mistakes he did share human weakness. He did not try and mask his tiredness at the Samaritan well, his distress at the grave of Lazarus, or his agony in the Garden of Gethsemane (John 4:6; 11:35; Matthew 26:38). The writer to the Hebrews says, 'We do not have a high priest who is unable to sympathise with our weaknesses, but we have one who has been tempted in every way, just as we are – yet was without sin' (Hebrews 4:15). Of course wisdom is needed in sharing mistakes and failure. It depends on the nature of the failure, how it is shared and the maturity of the group. It is one thing for church leaders to reveal passing doubts; it is another to publicise settled convictions that are at variance with fundamental Christian doctrines. It is one thing to apologise for impatience or shortness of temper, another to publicise a serious moral lapse. One important test is whether such sharing is 'edifying' – i.e. whether it helps in building up others in the faith. When Paul confessed his weakness and fear his aim was to testify to the Spirit's power (1 Corinthians 2:3–4; 2 Corinthians 12:7–10).

## The leader's authority

An emphasis on servant leadership may give the false impression that the leader is simply a doormat. Although Jesus was pre-eminently a servant of others, he exercised authority as part of this service. In giving himself as a servant of the poor he confronted with authority those who were exploiting them. He overturned the tables of the money-changers in the temple (John 2:13–16) and he did not mince words in criticising the Pharisees (Matthew 23:27). Similarly Paul was authoritative in rebuking immorality and doctrinal error (1 Corinthians 5:1–5; Galatians 1:9). While the modern leader does not have quite the same authority as Christ and the apostles it is important to note that Christians in the early church were exhorted 'Obey your leaders and submit to their authority' (Hebrews 13:17). In recent years church leaders have often failed to exercise the authority of discipline and as a result there has been an increase in moral laxity and heretical teaching. The house church movement has tried to redress the balance and re-emphasise church discipline. New members are expected to submit to 'discipling' by maturer Christians who in turn are discipled by senior members. Those at the top of the pyramid submit to one another. At its best the system can be beneficial, but it is open to abuse and some sections of the house church movement can fairly be accused of authoritarian leadership.[8] When the pendulum swings correction of one abuse can lead to another in the opposite direction. Authoritarian control can lead to

dependency and the test of all leadership is how effective it
is in promoting Christian maturity as opposed to childish
dependence. It is clear from the New Testament that there
are to be disciples of Jesus, but nowhere are we told to be
disciples of church leaders; we can say 'The Lord is my
shepherd' but not 'The shepherd is my lord'. The goal is an
adult dependence on Christ, not a childish dependence on a
human leader.

But what of New Testament commands to submit to and
obey our leaders? It is interesting to note that a strong word
for 'obey' (*peitharcheo* in the Greek) is used of obedience
to God and to civil authorities: 'We must obey God rather
than men!' (Acts 5:29) and 'Remind the people to be
subject to rulers and authorities, to be obedient' (Titus
3:1). On the other hand a weaker word (*peitho*) is used of
obedience to church leaders – 'Obey your leaders and
submit to their authority' (Hebrews 13:17). The context is
one of example, rather than of domineering – 'Remember
your leaders. . . . Consider the outcome of their way of life
and imitate their faith' (Hebrews 13:7). The focus is on
'Jesus Christ . . . the same yesterday and today and for
ever' (v 8). The weaker word (*peitho*) has the meaning of
being persuaded by, or being convinced by someone and it
suggests reasoned exhortation rather than an authoritarian
command. When Peter exhorts the younger leaders to
'submit' themselves to the older ones he uses a word which
literally means 'rank yourself under', and suggests therefore a readiness to respect the older ones rather than a
basic inferiority to them. He goes on to say that *all*
should act humbly towards each other and all should be
ready to humble themselves 'under God's mighty hand'
(1 Peter 5:5–6). As in Ephesians 5:21 submission is to be
mutual.

There was a danger that some would misuse their new-
found freedom in Christ to reject all authority. The writers
of the New Testament therefore had to emphasise the need
to respect leaders. There is the same need today in an age
when many share the mood of rebellion against authority,

but this is not the same as urging submission to an authoritarian leadership. Timothy is told 'Command and teach these things' (1 Timothy 4:11), but the word for 'command' (*parangelo*) has the idea of coming alongside to pass on a message. Timothy is later warned 'Do not rebuke an older man harshly, but exhort (*parakaleo*) him as if he were your father. Treat younger men as brothers' (1 Timothy 5:1). *Parakaleo* can also mean to encourage and is a word particularly associated with the ministry of the Holy Spirit, the divine paraclete. Encouragement rather than domination is to be the mark of the Christian leader. In 1 Timothy 4:6 Timothy's teaching task is described as 'laying before' (*hupotithemi*) his brethren Christian truths – there is no hint of dogmatic dictation. Paul instructs him: 'The Lord's servant must not quarrel. . . . Those who oppose him he must gently instruct' (2 Timothy 2:24–5).

John Tiller and Mark Birchall stress that 'authority for ministry is given by Christ to the whole church which recognises the particular gifts bestowed upon each individual including those who are to be appointed to any leadership function'.[9] It is important, however, to distinguish between the church's official recognition of a leader's authority on his appointment and the day-to-day acceptance of that authority by those who are being led. In practice the latter will come as trust develops; 'Authority comes from what you do, not from the office,' commented one vicar.[10]

## Suffering

The servant leader who stands up for truth, justice and righteousness is likely to experience suffering. The 'servant passages' in Isaiah come to a climax in chapter 53 with a prophecy of the sufferings of Christ – 'He carried our sorrows . . . He was oppressed and afflicted' (vv 4 and 7). Jesus described himself as the shepherd who gives his life for the sheep; when the wolf comes the shepherd must protect the sheep even at the cost of his own personal safety. We encountered a modern parallel in South Africa – a white church leader who experienced threatening telephone calls and even sabotage to his car because he had defended black leaders wrongly accused of terrorism. In some countries the Christian leader may even suffer martyrdom. 'It is worth remembering,' said Max Warren,[11] 'that no sixty years since the crucifixion have seen so many men and women being martyred because of their faith in the crucified.' Suffering is not always a matter of opposition or persecution, but may be a matter of criticism, frustration or of illness. Chapter 11 speaks of some of the stress caused by conflict. Often the leader who has suffered, however, will have a richer ministry to others who suffer. 'When you crush lavender you find its full fragrance; when you squeeze an orange you extract its sweet juice.'[12] Paul put it this way: 'Praise be to the God and Father of our Lord Jesus Christ, the Father of compassion and the God of all comfort, who comforts us in all our troubles, so that we can comfort those in any trouble with the comfort we ourselves have received from God' (2 Corinthians 1:3–4).

## 10  THE LEADER'S VISION

The need for vision, goals and objectives

Renewing the vision

Moving on and moving out

Optimism, pessimism and realism

Vision, voices and prophecies

Quarrying out objectives

Communicating the vision

The Christian leader must be a servant of others, but sometimes servant leadership is so over-emphasised that Christian leaders are diffident at the thought of taking a lead at all. It is good when 'one-man-band' leadership is replaced by 'enabling leadership', where the leader sees his task primarily as equipping others to serve, but it is disastrous when the word 'leadership' drops out and only the word 'enabling' is left. Unless the leader also communicates vision he simply becomes an 'enabling eunuch'; he ought to be a captain who gives direction and not just a referee who reacts to others' initiatives.[1] We have to ask 'What are people being enabled for?' 'What are the directions, purposes and goals?' We must not be so task-orientated that we forget the importance of people and their needs, but neither must we be so people-orientated that we forget the task and the goals. The captain of an aeroplane has to be concerned about the welfare of his passengers and crew, but it is even more important to know where he is going and to keep the plane on course.

## The need for vision

Many Old Testament leaders were fired up for their task through being given a vision. Moses saw a burning bush in the desert and learnt how God can transform the ordinary by the fire of his Spirit (Exodus 3:1–12). At a time of political turmoil and moral collapse Isaiah had a vision of the Lord on a throne and realised that God was in control in spite of appearances to the contrary (Isaiah 6). God spoke to Jeremiah through an almond tree and a cooking pot, giving him a vision of the power of his word in a day of disaster (Jeremiah 1). Both Moses and Jeremiah were diffident and complained that they lacked the gift of communication. They needed a vision of God's power and of his willingness and ability to equip his leaders.

Today's leaders equally need to spend time with God, but we are usually too busy and however much we pay lip service to the importance of prayer our diaries betray the fact that we think much time spent in prayer is time wasted. God is not in such a hurry as we are. Moses had to spend forty years in the desert before God was ready to call him, or before he was ready to be called. Ideally leaders should spend time in prayer as a group and not just individually. In addition to regular weekly or fortnightly meetings it is valuable to plan special 'retreats' once or twice a year to capture and renew the vision. Antioch became a missionary-sending church after its leaders spent time together in prayer and fasting (Acts 13:1–2). They were not only given a wider vision of God's plans, they were even shown which individuals were to be called to carry out those plans. We have so stressed individual calling today that we forget the need for the church or its leaders to act as the instruments of the Holy Spirit in calling others to service. Perhaps leaders should develop the habit of going up to individuals and saying 'We believe God may be calling you to. . . .' Too often we wait for volunteers.

We need a vision of God's power and of his willingness to equip his leaders, but we also need a vision of the needs of his people. Moses was well aware of the plight of Israel in Egypt and it is clear from the early chapters of Isaiah that the prophet was aware of the social and religious needs of the nation. Nehemiah was motivated to earnest prayer and action as soon as he received news of the disasters at Jerusalem (Nehemiah 1). Leaders today need to study the Bible and plan a regular pattern of Christian reading, but they also need to keep informed on what is happening in the locality and in the world. Paul Harvey has said, 'A blind man's world is bounded by the limits of his touch, an ignorant man's world by the limits of his knowledge and a great man's world by the limits of his vision.'[2] Too often leaders are limited in their vision by tradition or past experience. Peter needed new vision before he was prepared to bring the Gospel to the Gentiles (Acts 10:9–23).

Sometimes a vision has to be renewed. Jeremiah became disillusioned as he met opposition to his ministry, but after sharing his frustration with the Lord he was promised restoration, help and strength if only he would return to his task (Jeremiah 15:15–21). John the Baptist went through a period of doubt while in prison, but when he sent some of his disciples to share these doubts with Christ they brought back glowing reports of Christ's power in action (Matthew 11:2–6). In times of difficulty and distress it is vital to have a renewed vision of Christ's power and of his ultimate victory. 'The world is not moving on to chaos: it is moving on to Christ.'[3]

## A divine discontent

Leaders with vision are never content with the status quo but are always wanting to move on and move out to new opportunities. Both Jesus and Paul had a 'divine discontent'. In Mark 1 we see how Jesus' early ministry at Capernaum won an enthusiastic response – 'The whole town gathered at the door' (v 33) – but after an early morning period in prayer he refused to continue at Capernaum even though his disciples urged him to stay. He replied, 'Let us go on to the next towns, that I may preach there also; for that is why I came out' (v 38, RSV). Paul visited a large number of towns in Asia Minor and Europe, but far from being content he was eager to preach the Gospel in Rome (Romans 1:15) and in Spain (Romans 15:24). 'It has always been my ambition,' said Paul, 'to preach the gospel where Christ was not known' (Romans 15:20). He suffered from acute spiritual claustrophobia. Servant leadership can be misunderstood to mean that it is wrong to have ambition, but Gospel-centred ambition is good.

Not all are called to an itinerant ministry and there are usually agreed boundaries in the work of a local church. It can also be bewildering for a local congregation if its leadership changes course too quickly or too frequently or spills out new ideas before the old ones have been digested. Even within boundaries, however, there are often new possibilities to be explored. We must always be open to new guidance and new leading. 'The Spirit, despite our careful, elaborate ecclesiastical wind tunnels piously constructed for his benefit, still blows where and how he wills.'[4]

## Problems and possibilities

Leaders need vision in order to be possibility thinkers. After the people of Israel had left Egypt and had arrived on the edge of the Promised Land the Lord instructed Moses, 'Send some men to explore the land of Canaan, which I am giving to the Israelites. From each ancestral tribe send one of its leaders' (Numbers 13:2). After going up and down the land the spies reported back that the land was good and fruitful. However, the people were strong and the cities large and fortified. Two of the spies, Caleb and Joshua, focused on God's promises and urged the people to enter the land in reliance on God's strength. The other ten focused on the problems and urged a quick return to Egypt. It is a fascinating illustration of two kinds of leadership – the type that is overwhelmed by problems and the type that sees them as challenges to be overcome.

The visonary leader is not a false optimist who ignores or dismisses problems, but nor is he a pessimist who is crippled by them; he is a realist who sees the problems in the light of God's promises. Henry Kissinger once said, 'The great man understands the essence of a problem; the ordinary man sees only the symptoms. . . . The great man has a vision of the future which enables him to place obstacles into perspective; the ordinary leader turns pebbles in the road into boulders.'[5]

## How vision comes

The word 'vision' as applied to the modern leader does, of course, have a wider meaning than the literal visions seen by Old Testament prophets. Some have argued that dreams, prophecies, voices and visions are unnecessary or even misguided now that we have the written New Testament to guide us, but while their importance is now modified it is difficult to argue in the light of experience tested by scripture that they have no place at all today. In our present parish there are plans to convert a redundant church building into a local community centre and the vision for this arose from a 'picture' of the redundant church filled with people seen by a member of the congregation during a week-end house-party. This picture was tested by both the leaders and the congregation through discussion, prayer, the raising of money and the difficult task of obtaining building permission. Visions, pictures and prophecies can come from self and from Satan as well as from the Holy Spirit and they need testing through circumstances, advice and above all by scripture. Paul said, 'Do not put out the Spirit's fire; do not treat prophecies with contempt,' but he added, 'Test everything' (1 Thessalonians 5:19–21).[6] Leaders have to be open to the fact that God may choose to speak in a variety of ways and through different people. Sometimes a vision unfolds in a series of stages.

In Acts 16 we find Paul arriving at Derbe and Lystra. He then considers the next step in his journey, firstly planning to go through the province of Asia and then planning to enter Bithynia, but we are told that both these possibilities were ruled out by the Holy Spirit. It is not clear whether this was by special vision, by inner conviction or as the result of prayer and discussion. Finally he is given a vision of a man of Macedonia begging him 'Come over to Macedonia and help us', and so the Gospel enters Europe (Acts 16:6–10). But Paul was not always guided by special visions. His evangelistic mission at Philippi in Macedonia begins with a piece of strategic planning; on the Sabbath he goes outside the city gate to the river where he expects to find a group of Jewish women at prayer. From this group the first church is born in Europe (Acts 16:13–15). Paul's teaching ministry at Athens begins as a distress reaction in seeing the city full of idols, not as a result of some special vision (Acts 17:16–17).

Whether or not a strategy is worked out as a result of a literal vision, research is vital; just as the spies in Numbers 13 researched the Promised Land so church leaders will want to research their locality. A vision will be a false one if it fails to take into account the actual needs. In some housing areas, for example, the inhabitants grow older in unison, starting with an estate of young families and ending up several years later with an estate of senior citizens. It is no good having a vision of youth outreach if there are no young people in the area. Research will often give us vision by opening our eyes to whole sections of the population that are not being catered for. There may be a flourishing youth club but does it include young people of every social and intellectual category? Does the racial mix of the congregation match that of the population around? Vision is often broadened by exposure to other churches. Some years ago we wanted to start a pattern of family worship, but it was difficult for those who had never experienced such a pattern to evaluate the opportunities and the snags. The way through was to take a group to visit another church where family worship was established, and in this way they were able to experience it for themselves and to talk through the pros and cons with the leaders.

Vision is broadened too by exposure to churches in other lands. We may not belong to the ecclesiastical jet set, but we can read books, articles and prayer letters and talk with missionaries and overseas visitors. The church in England has been given fresh vision through the importing of church growth ideas from the United States, for example. Too often we have accepted static or declining numbers and have lacked the will to ask hard questions or to plan for growth. We were hosting a friend from South Africa, a black pastor who had undertaken a course in the United States and had then come across to London for a visit, and I gently explained that in England he would not find the large churches he had experienced in the United States. 'Don't worry,' he replied, 'our church in South Africa was founded by missionaries from England.' Neither the missionaries nor their South African converts had had a vision of significant church growth. By way of contrast the Liberation Theology of Latin America has much to teach us by its principle of relating the Bible to social issues.

## Spelling out the vision

Once the leadership group has a general vision of the way forward it needs to work out specific aims and objectives. It is one thing to research the locality but it is another to devise a plan of action. Engraved on a huge granite pillar by the grave of Karl Marx are his words 'The philosphers have only interpreted the world in various ways; the point, however, is to change it.' Too often the academic thinks he has resolved a problem once it has been analysed and labelled; a plan of action needs to be worked out in detail. John Adair advises, 'Quarry an objective out of an aim, then cut steps into the objectives.'[7]

Aims or objectives must be specific and they must be achievable. An unrealistic aim will only lead to frustration and disillusionment. A vicar in London who was planning a local mission told me, 'We are believing God for a hundred conversions!' The leadership group had reached the conviction that this was a realistic aim after a time of discussion and prayer. For some churches the figure of one hundred might be unrealistic. The aims and objectives should shape the organisation and structures rather than vice versa. The order should be as follows –

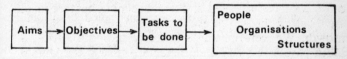

Too often the leadership in the church looks at the structures and organisations and then asks what the aims and objectives of the Youth Club, the Women's Meeting or the Men's Fellowship should be. But a more radical look at aims and objectives could suggest quite different structures; if one objective is to develop family life this might be better achieved by having organisations that cater for the whole family or at least for married couples rather than divide husband and wife into the Women's Meeting and the Men's Fellowship.

Progress in achieving aims and objectives must be regularly measured; one of the main tasks of a central leadership group in the systemic or organic style of leadership is the monitoring, modifying and developing of objectives (see pp. 24–7). When the leadership knows the vision and the aims there comes the task of communicating them to the whole church. Clear communication is one of the keys to good leadership and on major issues it will be wise to share the vision as widely as possible before a final decision is made. In this way mistakes can be avoided and the whole congregation will begin to 'own' the vision as theirs. Churches are usually good at communicating the vision when it comes to building projects; attractive brochures are produced, plans are explained and the stages spelt out carefully. They are not so good when it comes to mission strategy and a cynic would say that careful communication is used in building projects because money raising is involved; unless there is clear and compelling communication people will not give. Bishop John Taylor has commented, 'I have not heard recently of committee business being adjourned because those present were still awaiting the arrival of the Spirit of God. I have known projects abandoned for lack of funds, but not for lack of the gifts of the Spirit.'[8] It is equally important to have clear communication when evangelistic and social projects are envisaged; occasionally it may be right to take up the 'sermon slot' with an exposition of a new strategy or with a report on an established one. Just as missionaries share news with us on furlough, so the local missionaries need a chance to report on their strategy and progress. In many churches it is easy to sit in a pew Sunday after Sunday without ever discovering what the leadership strategy is.

It is also important that each church member is helped to see his or her role within the overall vision. Peter Wagner defines leadership as 'The ability to set goals in accordance with God's purpose for the future and to communicate those goals to others in such a way that they voluntarily and harmoniously work together to accomplish those goals for the glory of God'.[9] Olan Hendrix tells the story of a visitor coming to view the site of a new cathedral and speaking to two bricklayers, one of whom describes his task as 'laying bricks', the other as 'building a cathedral'; both answers were true, but only the second saw his work as an integral part of the overall vision.[10] In the British office of an international missionary society we found that the top executives could more easily see a relationship between their work and the advance of the Gospel in South America but it was more difficult for the secretaries immersed in typing and filing to do so. The daily prayer meeting was an opportunity to share news for praise and prayer, but we found the need to institute a regular, extended briefing in order to explain the goals and objectives of the overseas church and to report on progress.

## Enthusiasm

Goal setting must be followed by clear communication, but this communication must be accompanied by enthusiastic motivation. An absent-minded clergyman had forgotten the name of his new secretary and so uttered the following prayer during their first session together: 'Lord undertake for our sister in all the problems and burdens she faces.' Coming from a secular job and unfamiliar with the language of Zion the secretary responded afterwards with concern: 'I hope your sister will soon be all right.' Their first session lacked both clear communication and enthusiastic motivation. The English are not renowned for enthusiasm, except at football matches, and we are suspicious of the warmth and drive of our transatlantic friends. Disraeli once counselled Queen Victoria against appointing Bishop Tait as Archbishop of Canterbury – 'There is in his idiosyncrasy a strange fund of enthusiasm, a quality which ought never to be possessed by an Archbishop of Canterbury or a Prime Minister of England.' To be fair the word 'enthusiasm' had a more specialist meaning in those days, but it is nevertheless true that both then and now it is often considered 'bad form' to be enthusiastic about the Christian faith.

Field-Marshal Montgomery had a special gift for the enthusiastic motivation of others and described the gift of leadership as 'The capacity and will to rally men and women to a common purpose, and the character which will inspire confidence. The leader must have infectious optimism and the determination to persevere in the face of difficulties. He must also radiate confidence.'[11] He always

believed that the test of a leader was whether you left at the
end of an interview with a new confidence and a clear idea
as to what needed to be done.

We were at a Christian conference centre in the North of
England and I had rashly volunteered to join an advertised
walk. We had driven to the end of a valley in order to start
the walk, but as it was pelting with rain we were huddled in
the car discussing whether there would be loss of face if we
crept back to the conference centre. Suddenly the leader
appeared at the car window; 'Let's go,' she said. She was
right. The walk was planned, we had volunteered to go on
it, and the weather was beginning to improve. Now was not
the time for vacillating discussion. After all the prayer and
plans there comes the time when the leader's next task is to
say 'Let's go!' Enthusiasm literally means 'God breathed'
and it is therefore a quality that needs to be generated by
the Holy Spirit, not worked up by human effort. Timothy
had many good qualities, but he suffered from diffidence
and was not by nature a man who would find it easy to
enthuse others. 'Fan into flame the gift of God, which is in
you through the laying on of my hands,' Paul advises him,
'For God did not give us a spirit of timidity, but a spirit of
power, of love and of self-discipline' (2 Timothy 1:6–7).
Whether by pictures or prophecies or through the more
mundane channels of research, discussion and advice, the
Holy Spirit is the secret of vision and enthusiasm for
Christian leaders.

# 11    CHANGE AND CONFLICT

The need for change

Factors resisting change

The different approaches to change

Conflict – the hidden factors

Management of conflict – avoidance,
                                confrontation,
                                coercion,
                                compromise or
                                co-operation

'Make all the changes you can during the first six months while you're still in the honeymoon phase.' This was the advice given during college training to John Harris, a North American minister.[1] The advice I was given was diametrically opposite – 'Don't make any changes in your first year; take time to assess the needs.' The interesting and disturbing assumption in both these quotations is that the pace and timing of change is the responsibility of the newly arrived, one-man, omnicompetent leader. Whatever the right pace, method and direction of change – and this will vary according to the circumstances – Christian leaders with vision will want to make changes. There may be the need to develop different styles of worship or to promote a greater concern for evangelism and social action. It may be that the congregation are moving in the right direction, but the time has come to change gear.

## The Gospel means change

Although the Gospel means change, Christians often seem to resist it. Those who are conservative in theology are tempted to be conservative towards new ideas. The famous hymn 'Abide with me' includes the lines

> Change and decay in all around I see
> O Thou who changest not abide with me.

Linking change to decay implies that it is usually bad and that the Christian must take refuge from a changing and threatening world in an unchanging God. It is true that 'Jesus Christ is the same yesterday and today and for ever' (Hebrews 13:8), but this sameness is one of character, promises and purpose and that purpose is to save and change the world. The work of the Holy Spirit is to change Christians into Christ's likeness 'with ever-increasing glory' (2 Corinthians 3:18). The church is to 'grow up in every way . . . into Christ' (Ephesians 4:15 RSV) and is to be a change agent in society so that God's plan of uniting all things in Christ can be fulfilled (Ephesians 1:10). The culmination of God's work is 'a new heaven and a new earth' (Revelation 21:1). The Christian leader's task therefore is to promote change according to God's plan – change in himself, in the church and in the world at large.

### Management of change

The different styles of leadership described in Chapter 1 have a typically varied set of responses to the need for change. The *traditional* leader wants to preserve continuity with the past and so tends to resist change. The positive value of this stance is that traditional leaders are not easily blown in every direction by changing fashions in doctrine, liturgy and architecture. They can be counted on to evaluate carefully new ideas in theology and morals; this is an important safeguard when standards are in decline, though the traditionalist is usually too quick to assume that they are. The danger of this approach is that 'it gathers round it other forces of conservatism which have no necessary connection with the purpose of the church. The influence of people who are concerned with the preservation of ancient buildings is very noticeable in the Church of England.'[2] The same can be said about the preservation of Elizabethan English. In a fast-changing society a church which has this kind of leadership can quickly become irrelevant and therefore ineffective. A huge Victorian church with seating for over a thousand and a pipe organ geared for highbrow concerts is not likely to cut much ice in the inner city unless considerable adaptation is allowed and welcomed. Traditional values play a large part in committees set up to vet changes in church furnishings; one such committee member argued for the preservation of a decaying pipe organ in an inner city area because it was 'so like the one we had in India'.

The *charismatic* leader will welcome change and in a time of social upheaval his leadership can harness the forces of change to give clear goals and purpose. This may be the right approach where a church's life has become moribund and, for example, new forms of worship are needed in order to attract families. If the previous minister stayed a long time, perhaps up to retirement, and church life got into a rut a new minister may find on arrival that the congregation are longing for a new approach and will welcome rapid and radical change. But the charismatic style is the way of revolution rather than evolution and can be too abrupt. The temptation for this kind of leader is to be impatient with committees, to take a strong lead without sharing decisions and to ignore or override people's wishes. As a result there may develop an attitude of detachment – 'the minister doesn't listen to us, so let him get on with it' – or of dependence; those who do not want an authoritarian style will leave after a period of conflict and only dependent church members will be left.

*Classical* leadership plans for change by a series of

organised stages. This has advantages over the charismatic style and makes careful consultation and preparation possible, but the process may take so long that the finished result is out of date before it has been completed. A secular example is the M25 motorway around London which has been inadequate for the volume of traffic ever since it opened. Within the Church of England, liturgical revision took the form of a series of experimental booklets, but unfortunately this process was not allowed to continue and ended in the production of a large and unwieldy 'permanent' book which bids fair to fossilise worship in 1950s language. As a notice in a vestry pithily expressed it, 'change is here to stay.'

The *human relations* leader on the other hand majors on the need to help church members adjust to change in society around. He will provide double glazing for villagers who are deafened by the roar of an increasing number of lorries. Other styles of leadership will seek to campaign for a by-pass.

The *systemic* or organic approach is to make provision for continuous adaptation or change; this style is one of evolution as opposed to the charismatic one of revolution. There are two main factors giving impetus to change – the purpose and goals of the church and the state of society around. The type of population in the area may alter over a period of time – a council housing estate may begin its life with young families and end with senior citizens before starting the cycle again, or there may be a process of 'gentrification' as professional families move into what were traditionally working-class areas. The local church will have to take these factors into account in planning its programme. On the other hand the goal of creating and developing fellowship may lead to building a church lounge whatever the situation in the local community. Logically this style should require temporary or semi-permanent rather than permanent buildings.

## Factors affecting attitudes to change

As people grow older they tend to find change more difficult, though there are some personalities of all ages who welcome change. The wise leader will be sensitive to these factors and not label caution and nervousness as obstinacy. Some years ago we introduced a more modern service at our midweek Communion. The elderly ladies present were thoroughly bewildered and disorientated; they did not know when to stand up and when to sit down. Perhaps we had not prepared for change with sufficient care, but even if we had there would still have been difficulties in making the adjustment. In his book *Future Shock* Alvin Tofler demonstrated that we are living in an era of accelerated change.[3] The result is that many people look to the church as a sanctuary where nothing changes; they want it to act as a windbreak against the forces that threaten to disrupt their lives. This attitude may be found also among occasional worshippers who expect traditional worship at Christmas and Easter or among non-worshippers who object to the removal of the familiar church on the corner. The task of the Christian leader is to wean people from dependence on an unchanging church life to dependence on an unchanging God. The ideal model is that of a pilgrim people whose God is a constant companion 'through all the changing scenes of life'. This 'frees us from the feeling of having to control life, from having to live defensively against change'.[4] In practice it will usually be wise to change gear gradually and carefully. If change is introduced slowly at first then the climate will be favourable to an increased pace of change later; it is the movement from inertia to five miles an hour that requires the most effort. Leaders will often be faced with an older generation who have problems in adapting to change and a younger generation who are pressing for it; they need to help each group to understand the other. In addition to factors of age, personality and social upheaval there may be an underlying insecurity or other psychological factors behind resistance to change. We shall discuss this when we come to look at the hidden factors in conflict, below. The leader will need to recognise these factors in himself as well as in others.

## Change and conflict

Change may lead to confrontation and conflict. John the Baptist described the crowds who came to hear him as a 'brood of vipers' (Luke 3:7) and did not hesitate to challenge Herod's moral laxity. Jesus entered into conflict with the religious leaders of his day; he did not compliment them on 'contributing a valuable insight into current theological debate',[5] but called them 'blind guides', 'hypocrites' and 'whitewashed tombs' (Matthew 23:13, 16 and 27). The price for both John and Jesus of change, confrontation and conflict was death. Again the task of taking the Gospel beyond the Jewish people to the Gentiles was only accomplished after conflict. At one point Peter retracted and stopped sharing meals with Gentiles; Paul 'opposed him to his face' (Galatians 2:11). Clearly some issues are so important that we have to be prepared for confrontation and conflict. At the same time we have to be careful not to enter controversy on secondary matters; 'Don't have anything to do with foolish and stupid arguments,' wrote Paul, 'you know they produce quarrels' (2 Timothy 2:23). There is a certain kind of personality that enjoys conflict and even seeks it.

### Hidden factors in conflict

We are all at different points on a spectrum when it comes to argument. Some of us relish it, some run away from it and most of us find it difficult. If there is a sudden outburst in a discussion group some will sit on the edge of their chairs in excitement as if they have been given free seats near a boxing ring. Others will shrink back and wriggle uncomfortably. It is important for the leader to know his own make-up and to understand the reasons behind his attitude to conflict. There may be factors in childhood or adolescence causing hidden insecurity. In some this insecurity will lead to avoidance of conflict because they cannot cope with the emotional trauma; for them it will be peace at any price. Others will react in the opposite way by choosing confrontation rather than avoidance; their insecurity will make it difficult to engage in the emotional turmoil of a protracted debate and they will cope with conflict by laying down the law in an authoritarian manner. The leader will need to recognise that conflict within church circles may be sparked off by external factors. A business executive may inexplicably explode over a minor point on the church committee agenda; he may have had a frustrating day at the office or may be coping with the fear of redundancy. A secretary who feels that her work has not been adequately appreciated by her boss may make her presence felt by niggling over minor points in the minutes.

There may be different causes within church life itself. A congregation which has been forced through too rapid a pace of change may react by digging in their heels on some surprising minor point; when there has been a build-up of frustration the lid is bound to blow off. Ministers may be affected by external factors, too. Now that part of their traditional role has been taken over by doctors, psychiatrists and social workers some experience an 'identity crisis' leading to self-doubt, insecurity and fear of criticism, making it difficult to promote change and so risk conflict. Where a local church committee has the right to 'hire and fire' the minister, he may be inhibited from risking conflict. One chaplaincy church overseas fired their minister because he was too successful in attracting local nationals to the church; there was a fear that the British might be outnumbered on the church committee and too many services conducted in the local language.

## Management of conflict

Management of conflict will differ according to the style of leadership and there are close parallels to the different attitudes to change. The first one to mention is *avoidance* and is the one favoured by the traditional leader who will try to avoid conflict because it threatens to undermine the congregation's harmony and stability. This style tends to be symptom-solving and not problem-solving. In many marriages and fellowships there are certain subjects that are regarded as taboo because it is known that differences exist and there is too much fear of conflict to allow them to be brought out into the open. In a congregation these subjects may include infant baptism, the use of charismatic gifts, race relations and political issues. A marriage or fellowship where differences are not aired, however, is likely to be stale and stagnant. The traditional leader may try to stifle debate by saying 'Let's pray about it and ask the Lord to preserve our unity.' Prayer is obviously a vital weapon in resolving conflict but it should never be used as a broom to sweep issues under the carpet, nor should a call to unity be used as a blackmail device to prevent open discussion.

There are various other methods used in the secular world to avoid conflict and some of them are not unknown in the church. Difficult items may be put low down on the agenda so that there is never time to deal with them or they may be left off altogether. Discussion may be deferred until 'some more appropriate time' or a working party may be set up to research the problem in the hope that the issue may have been defused or forgotten by the time it reports back. Some will give verbal assent to a difficult proposal but never get round to putting it into practice. On the other hand there will be occasions when avoidance is quite legitimate – tempers may be too high, there may not be time for careful discussion or there may genuinely be a need for a working party to research the issue. Finally, the issue may not be sufficiently important to justify conflict or the degree of conflict likely to arise may be out of proportion to its importance. Leaders who are undertaking a programme of change are unwise to fight on all fronts at once and a readiness to give in on minor issues may make it easier to promote major ones.

The second approach is *confrontation* and is the one favoured by the charismatic leader who welcomes conflict and thrives on it. It is an opportunity to rally his supporters to fight a common cause. His use of confrontation may increase the conflict, harden attitudes and make it more difficult to resolve. Launching an attack on opponents by letter or public statement may only force them to erect stronger defences; I have seen this happen as a village vicar threw thunderbolts from the pulpit. It is usually wise to talk privately with individuals or groups who are said to disagree. We may find there are misunderstandings on both sides and Satan loves to increase polarisation by letting each side get a distorted picture of the other's position. However, there will be occasions once positions have been clarified where confrontation is unavoidable. This as we saw was the case with Paul and Peter (Galatians 2:11). We must be clear that the issue is one of fundamental principle such as immorality or racial injustice and even then dialogue and persuasion are helpful preliminaries – 'A gentle answer turns away wrath' (Proverbs 15:1). When it comes to an international or national issue the confrontational style of the charismatic leader may be particularly valuable. He will be able to launch a crusade to change policies on international trade, or the sale of arms.

The third possibility is *coercion*, the approach typical of authoritarian classical leadership. 'I simply tell them that the conduct of worship is my prerogative,' said one minister. It is possible for a leader to use his position, status or authority in order to pre-empt discussion. He may do this by quoting scripture, church law or tradition without recognising or making it clear that his interpretation could be called in question. Similarly a member of the church may be given a word of prophecy, a vision or a picture which they share in such a way as to end discussion. It is usually wise for the leadership of the church to test, evaluate and interpret prophecies and pictures before taking them as ultimate guidance. The balance given us in 1 Thessalonians is 'Do not put out the Spirit's fire' (5:19), 'Test everything' (5:21). The threat of resignation is another example of coercion: 'If you use that teaching programme I am going to give up as a Sunday school teacher' or 'If you start using that hymn book I shall stop coming.' If after discussion the person refuses to withdraw the threat it may be wise to accept the resignation. Otherwise the church leadership is put into a blackmail position that could easily be repeated on more minor issues.

Coercion should be avoided wherever possible as it is likely to result either in greater conflict or in the build-up of resentment. On some occasions it is unavoidable. If a person's work is unsatisfactory it may be necessary to terminate their employment or threaten to do so when all other means of persuasion have failed.

The fourth possibility is *compromise*, the one favoured by the human relations leader, who is more concerned to promote happy relationships than to work out effective policies for mission. Many churches compromise by having a mixture of traditional and modern services. One church committee in the South East could not arrive at unanimity on whether to replace the pews with chairs in order to make possible greater flexibility in worship. They ended up by replacing the pews in the side aisles but not in the centre. This illustrates the difficulty with compromise; the leadership may end up by pleasing no one and may fail to establish an effective policy. A mixture of services may balance the competing needs of the older and younger generations in the church, but Elizabethan English will always be a barrier to newcomers even if it is only used once a month. If agreement cannot be reached it may be better to defer a decision rather than compromise, unless the compromise is seen as a temporary expedient.

## Co-operation is the ideal

We have seen that there are occasions when it is right to avoid conflict or to use confrontation, compromise or even coercion. What matters more than anything else is that the Christian leader should understand the pros and cons of each approach and recognise both the outward and hidden factors in his choice of style.[6] The ideal process, however, is one of *co-operation* where the parties involved work together not just to resolve the conflict but to use it in order to make progress. This is the systemic or organic style which seeks to harness the creative elements in conflict. Joyce Huggett has described how conflict can be 'a skilled teacher, a wise counsellor, a proficient life-transforming friend' and is 'an integral part of all close friendships'.[7]

One of God's leaders in the Old Testament was Jacob, a man with a character that needed a great deal of reshaping. His early style was one of cunning manipulation. Jacob found his years with Laban a frustrating time of conflict, but it was used to transform him and equip him for more effective leadership. He struck a bargain to serve his uncle Laban for seven years in return for the promise of Laban's daughter Rachel as his wife. At the end of the seven years his uncle gave him his other daughter Leah under cover of darkness so that Jacob unwittingly took her instead. It was a replay of Jacob's earlier cheating of his brother and so Jacob was brought face to face with a mirror image of his own cunning (Genesis 29:15–30). 'God is more concerned with spiritual growth than temporal comfort. . . . We greatly over-estimate the influence of "nice" people and what they can do for us. As a rule the other sort are far more important for us.'[8]

What is true for individuals can also be true for congregations. A time of conflict handled in the right way can be a time of growth – in openness, understanding and maturity. 'Tension,' says John Harris, 'is not a negative state; it is the positive precondition of renewal and rebirth in all organised forms of life.' Congregations which lack conflict are 'distant and polite, but without zest, spirit and strong affection'.[9]

What are the practical steps a leader needs to take in a situation of conflict? The first is *prayer*, an opportunity for the leader to release feelings of anger and bitterness at the foot of the cross and to ask for cleansing, wisdom, graciousness and courage. Through prayer comes the next step of *understanding*, as the leader begins to recognise the hidden factors behind the conflict both in himself and in others. The parable of the mote and beam may be appropriate here. Next the leader will need to *talk* with the individual or the group concerned and this will lead to greater understanding. It is the only way to clear up misunderstanding and to find out the other person's real position. 'Why has Mrs Smith stopped coming? Is she really as upset by the new services as the organist suggests?' It is important not to rely on third-party information. The fourth step is only to be taken when the third one has been unproductive and that is to *share* the problem with a wider group. In Matthew 18 Jesus gives advice on the steps to be taken in conflict, though it must be emphasised that the context is one where the other person is clearly in the wrong. 'If your brother sins against you, go and show him his fault, just between the two of you . . . if he will not listen, take one or two others along . . . if he refuses to listen to them, tell it to the church' (vv 15–17). This procedure would be appropriate in the case of immorality, heresy or a severe breakdown in relationships, but the principle of talking with the individual concerned before sharing the problem more widely is appropriate in nearly every case. Finally a *decision* needs to be made as to the right style or approach in resolving the conflict – is it to be confrontation, coercion, compromise or co-operation?

Conflict is not always the result of obvious sin on one or both sides. It may arise because there are simply differences of opinion over policies and programmes. There may be arguments over a new appointment, a new method of teaching or a new form of outreach. One co-operative approach is to set up a working group which includes representatives from all sides, though it may be wise to exclude at this stage the more extreme or intransigent – this is a matter of assessment. A smaller group can allow for greater freedom of expression in a relaxed atmosphere; in a bigger meeting where a large number of people are pressing to express their views there is a tendency for individuals to express themselves more forcefully in order to gain a hearing. The greater time available to a working group will facilitate growth in understanding and respect for each other's point of view. This group can then circulate a report to the full church committee prior to one of its meetings. Even if the report is not unanimous it can clarify the issues, remove misunderstandings and relax the tension. It is important that such a report should be relatively brief, clear and present both pros and cons of the policies being discussed. Sometimes conflict arises because committee members feel they are being steam-rollered and will therefore dig in their heels. They will relax more if they feel that their viewpoints are being given careful consideration and not being dismissed out of hand. There is always the risk that circulating a report in advance will lead to lobbying or to a hardening of attitude. More often, however, it will allow potential opponents of a scheme to experience an initial reaction that may be negative or even angry in the privacy of their own homes; after further reflection they may come to a point of greater openness. If the angry reaction takes place at the main church committee there is likely to be embarrassment and a hardening of attitude; opponents of the scheme may become defensive and find it difficult to withdraw from their positions.

One of the difficulties of presenting a scheme for change is that the congregation or church committee may have no experience of what is being proposed. It is often valuable to arrange visits to other churches where a new layout or form of service is in use. Another approach is to plan a period of experimentation followed by evaluation. This is useful as a way of defusing conflict, but experimentation has its hazards. It takes time to adjust to changes in worship and

the period of experimentation may end before this adjustment has taken place. If it is a case of changing the interior
layout of a church the temporary rearrangement may be
unsightly or unattractive. The advocates of change need to
argue persuasively but not too persuasively. It can be
counter-productive to overstate a case and it is a lack of
integrity to denigrate or misrepresent the views of others. It
is possible to win a battle but to lose support. I remember
watching a brilliant young minister advocating a case for
change; he piled up argument after argument and totally
demolished his opponents. But such is British concern for
the underdog that while his logic was impeccable he
increased support and sympathy for the other side.

Perhaps the biggest conflict in New Testament times was
over the question of whether Gentiles should be allowed to
become members of the church and, if so, under what
conditions. (This is referred to on p. 64.) Some Christians
from a Pharisee background demanded that Gentiles
should only be admitted if they were circumcised and
charged to 'obey the law of Moses' (Acts 15:5). There was
'sharp dispute and debate' at Antioch over this issue and it
could easily have split the church. There are lessons to be
learnt from the way the debate was handled. In order to
avoid a split between Antioch and Jerusalem Paul and
Barnabas were sent to Jerusalem to present the issue before
a meeting of the apostles and elders. It would have been
easy for views to polarise, but the early church provided for
a co-operative approach in resolving the conflict. After a
good deal of debate Peter stated the principle that such a
yoke should not be put on the necks of Gentile converts as
both Jew and Gentile are 'saved through grace' and not by
observing Jewish ceremonial laws. This was clearly a fundamental principle over which there could be no compromise. James summed up by supporting Peter but suggested
that Gentile believers be asked to respect the scruples of
their Jewish brethren by avoiding the eating of meat which
had idolatrous associations or from which the blood had not
been properly drained.[10] Paul makes a similar suggestion in

Romans 14; while the Christian is 'free' to eat meat that has been offered to idols he should refrain from doing so if it causes offence or becomes a stumbling-block to other Christians.

The Acts 15 debate gives instructive examples of confrontation followed by a co-operation that included compromise. This compromise was not one of fundamental principle but of practical application. It is not always easy to distinguish the two. Supposing there is a proposal to bring the Communion table away from the east wall of the church and into the centre. There are undoubtedly fundamental principles involved arising from our understanding of Communion, but the exact location of the table and the timing of the change can be seen as matters of practical application. There may well be need for a period of experimentation before the final decision is made.

# 12  LEADERSHIP DEVELOPMENT

It is debatable which is the best word to use for preparing leaders; 'teaching' sounds too academic and 'training' too activist. The word 'development' has the advantage that it can include spiritual, intellectual and practical aspects as well as learning to create good relationships, and it suggests a continuing process. Jesus is the model of development and in Luke 2 we read that he 'grew in wisdom and stature, and in favour with God and men' (v 52). The word 'Jesus' is the word for salvation (*yash'a*) used in the Old Testament and Michael Green defines salvation as 'bringing into a spacious environment . . . free to develop'.[1] Jesus' relationship to his disciples is also a model for the development of leadership. 'Follow me,' he tells the first disciples, 'and I will make you fishers of men' (Mark 1:17). The secret of their preparation was to share the whole of life with Jesus, to hear him teaching, to watch him healing, to note the quality of his life and to be sent out by him in ministry and mission. To some extent the relationship of Jesus and the twelve was patterned on the Jewish rabbi and his students, but the life of a rabbinic student was mainly limited to study, lectures and discussion, while for the twelve teaching and discussion took place in the context of active ministry. In the twentieth-century church preparation for ministry is usually more rabbinic than Christian and has often been centred on a residential theological college of monastic pattern. Even those colleges that have prided themselves on a biblical basis have produced training programmes that are biblical in content rather than methodology. It is fatally easy, however, to caricature and criticise theological colleges; many changes have taken place in recent years and they tend to be the whipping boys for the failures of the church. Whenever a defect in church life is identified it is attributed to faults in theological college training and the remedy is to add further sections to the syllabus without suggesting what can be deleted to make room for them. Resources are limited and the staff-student ratio such that there has to be an over-dependence on lectures rather than on seminars and tutorials. The danger is that those entering the professional ministry may unconsciously reproduce the environment of their theological college life and a crowded time-table in college with little time for unhurried reflection may lead to a frantic programme in the parish, while the lecture style in college may be continued in the pulpit; the new minister may be inexperienced or hesitant about using other approaches to teaching and learning. Changes are, however, taking place, questions are being asked and new experiments in training and development have been started.[2] It will be helpful to look at the principles and some of the recent developments as follows:

*Principles of leadership development*

- for every leader
- for shared leadership
- in practice and theory
- in mission and ministry
- in formation and information
- in context and community

# Development for every leader

Ideally leadership development should be available for potential leaders from all backgrounds and not just for the middle class or for the paid professional. One criticism made of the theological colleges in the past was that they became theological Sandhursts producing an elitist officer class that became distanced by status and training from

other ranks. A number of part-time training courses have
been started, providing sessions at evenings and at week-
ends in order to make leadership training available to men
and women from all walks of life. However, church authorities have demanded the same academic standards as the
colleges and most of those completing such courses are in
professional, managerial or administrative posts.[3]

In recent years there have been new experiments and one
Church of England Diocese has a Ministerial Training
Course which caters for a wide range of leaders, not all of
whom are destined for the professional ministry. Another
has a course entitled Group for Urban Ministry and
Leadership (GUML) which draws groups of ordinary church
members from congregations in Urban Priority Areas.
Many churches in the third world have discovered that they
cannot afford residential theological colleges and have
therefore developed a system of Theological Education by
Extension (TEE). TEE courses are produced centrally, but
teaching takes place in the local church or in a group of
churches under the guidance of a local tutor; in this way the
college comes to the student, rather than the student to the
college. It has the advantage that all the potential leaders in
a congregation can be included and leadership development can then be a continuing experience that goes on
beyond accreditation or ordination; the division between
professional and non-professional becomes blurred. Several theological colleges in Britain are offering correspondence courses on a 'TEE' label, though strictly speaking, as
there is no local tutor involved the label is inaccurate.
Maybe this is a development that will come later and it is
certainly a move in the right direction to make theological
colleges resource centres for a leadership explosion at all
levels.[4]

While there is a need to release more resources for the
training of professionals there is an even greater need for
resources for the training of other leaders. John Tiller and
Mark Birchall comment, 'The ministry of the laity as the
true Christian priesthood is quite overshadowed by the

small minority who compose the clergy, who have spent on them an overwhelming proportion of the funds raised to train and to maintain the church's ministry.'[5] At a medical and agricultural development conference in Kenya we were told that precious financial resources were going into training a small number of highly qualified doctors whereas there was an even greater need for a large number of health workers able to promote primary health care. Similarly large sums of money were going to complex and costly procedures for the few – such as open heart surgery and renal dialysis – whereas money was more urgently needed to provide basic preventive medicine for the many.

Are there parallels with leadership development and training for ministry? We need our specialists, but should they be seen as consultants and more resources be released for training a large number of primary leaders? Perhaps what is needed is a primary course available for many, from which a few will go on to secondary, more specialist training. To put it succinctly, should not training for primary ministry be seen as primary?

## Development for shared leadership

We saw from Chapter 5 that New Testament leadership was shared leadership. One of the many strengths of a theological college is that it provides a setting where students from different backgrounds learn to adapt to one another and live in community. But this is not the same as working as a team, and it is still possible for students to emerge as individualists. While the GUML course described opposite is not a residential community it has the strength that a group from the same parish is trained as a team, enabling the less confident to draw on the support of others.[6] What is more, the vicar or minister of each parish is involved in the programme and has to guarantee a role for the group once the first stage of the course is finished. Both the methodology and the goal of GUML are different from traditional courses and its aim is not to produce individualists, but teams. This goal is also possible in theory, if not always in practice, with TEE courses.

One of the skills needed in leaders is the ability to build and maintain a team. A recent paper by the Advisory Council for the Church's Ministry of the Church of England describes the task of the ordained minister as 'recognising, co-ordinating and distributing the ministry of others'.[7] This is the skill of the organiser described on pages 62–70, but it is not an experience that is traditionally part of training courses. 'If I hadn't been trained in the RAF on how to manage a unit,' commented a Midlands vicar, 'renewal wouldn't have happened in this parish in the way it has. Part of enabling is setting things up so that they happen.' James Anderson and Ezra Jones describe a floundering Christian leader in these words: 'His training had not prepared him for translating theological values into leadership decisions.'[8] Perhaps this skill is one that can only be learnt after a course is finished, or perhaps church authorities should only select for ordination those who have proved their ability to build a team. The ideal, however, would be to give opportunity for developing this skill during training.

## Practice and theory

The Archbishop of Canterbury has said, 'Much of the dissatisfaction that currently exists comes from the belief that present patterns of training are either too academic or at least too influenced by university models.'[9] The opposite danger is to produce skilled practitioners who are unreflective and anti-intellectual. The ideal is to develop training programmes that integrate practice and theory, action and reflection. As we saw on pages 86–7, Jesus' method was to teach, then demonstrate; the disciples then went into action themselves and their action was followed by reflection and discussion. 'Unlike some teachers the approach of Jesus was not intellectual or cerebral. It was not programmed or systematic but spontaneous and arising out of real-life situations.'[10] A walk through the grainfields, for example, leads to a debate about Sabbath observance (Matthew 12:1–8). Similarly Barnabas developed Paul's gifts by inviting him to join in his teaching ministry at Antioch (Acts 11:19–26) (see p. 72). Paul developed simultaneously in theological understanding and in pastoral experience. Many colleges and courses would like to develop their training programmes in an action/reflection direction, but are shackled by a crowded syllabus and limited resources. At the same time the opportunity to use university facilities brings pressure to make training even more academic in order to gain recognition by the Council for National Academic Awards. Hence the Archbishop's comments. Colleges are also shackled by student expectations and those which fail to attract students may fail to survive financially; whatever the advantages of a 'free market' it can also have its limitations. There is a need for academic excellence but the ideal would be to encourage co-ordination between colleges and courses leading to specialisation so that primary action/reflection modules are available to all and academic and other specialist modules are made available at a secondary level for those who are destined to go on to become specialist consultants.

In the past it has been argued that academic teaching should take place in college and practical training during the early years of ministry. The danger of this approach is that the professional minister who has not learnt to relate practice and theory in college will find it difficult to do so in a local church; his training programmes will have an academic rather than an action/reflection style. This approach also raises questions about the nature of theology; is it a series of timeless truths to be dispensed 'six foot above contradiction' or is it a group voyage of discovery in order to discern God's activity in the world and relate it to the Christian tradition? As we saw in Chapter 2 we have much to learn from Liberation Theology and the base communities (pp. 32–3). A minister who had been ordained for a number of years described the culture shock of moving from a law course to a theological college. 'In the law course we were trained to debate and discuss in group tutorials by studying actual cases and relating legal principles to them. There are parallels in medical student training. In the theological college we had days crowded with lectures with little opportunity or encouragement to reflect or debate. The aim of the course seemed to be one of pumping the maximum of information into the students rather than developing their capacity to think theologically about the issues facing them and others.' A lawyer does not memorise every detail of the law, but he is trained to think creatively from principle to practice. This is not a criticism of theological colleges, who are often victims of circumstances beyond their control; many have moved a long way since the days described above. Many would move further were it not for the shackles of a crowded syllabus and limited resources. Those courses which are free from such shackles are experimenting in a number of ways. One student on a ministerial training scheme found herself driving a London Underground train as part of a 'work' module which integrated practical experience into study and discussion on the teaching of scripture and tradition about the nature of work.

At local church level there are a variety of opportunities for combining action and reflection. A couple who ran an 'enquiry group' for their neighbours were motivated to research answers to the questions raised. Ministers who invite established couples to help them in baptism preparation have the opportunity to explain and relate the theology of baptism to practical Christian living. Training in counselling, in leading house groups and in door-to-door visiting gives added opportunity for action and reflection. An annual event such as a holiday club for children gives scope for specific training in a variety of skills. Of course there are some areas of theology which may not automatically surface from current issues or from the action/reflection approach; professional ministers will need to undertake careful monitoring to see that gaps are filled.

## Mission and ministry

We saw from Chapter 8 that too often professional and non-professional ministry has been seen as ministry 'in the temple'. There is, of course, a very necessary and proper temple ministry that includes the equipping of the people of God for service in the world. But all too often leaders are developed for ministry and not for mission. God's mission in and through the church to the world should provide the aims and objectives as well as affect the context and content of leadership training. A proportion of our training programmes should, for example, help Christian leaders to think and act creatively in the world of work. The agenda of the base community leader will include a large number of social issues while an emerging Pentecostal leader in Chile may not be allowed to become a pastor until he has planted a new congregation (see pp. 31–3).

## Formation and information

What the leader *is* in his life and example is just as important as what he *knows*. Whether at college level or at local church level development must be personal as well as intellectual. We have seen that the servant leader is to teach by example (p. 130) as well as by word; Paul tells Timothy to deal firmly with false doctrine, but the goal is love (1 Timothy 1:3–5). He himself is 'to set an example . . . in speech, in life, in love, in faith and in purity' (4:12). The Ephesian elders are warned, 'Take heed to yourselves and to all the flock' (Acts 20:28 RSV). The Pentecostal pastor Juan Carlos Ortiz used to combine central teaching on the family with visits to members' homes in order to see how the teaching was being applied (see p. 18).

The railway line diagram demonstrates how the various elements of leadership training need to be related. It illustrates a Theological Education by Extension programme which combines practical experience and study at home with spiritual formation; the seminars are the key to linking the three. A residential community such as a theological college can be more effective in promoting spiritual formation and helping students to develop their prayer life, their ability to make good relationships and their recognition and use of latent gifts. At local church level the elders' group and ideally every house group can become a greenhouse for spiritual formation. This is more likely to happen if members are prepared to spend a good deal of time together in study, recreation, prayer and action.

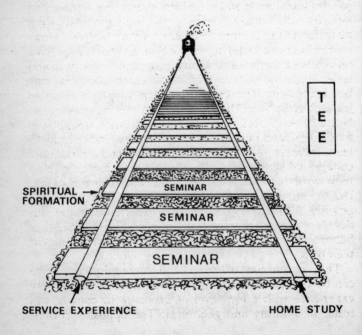

T E E

SPIRITUAL FORMATION → SEMINAR

SEMINAR

SEMINAR

SERVICE EXPERIENCE          HOME STUDY

## Context and community

Moving to live in an inner city area was a revolutionary experience for our family. It forced me to rethink the nature of the Gospel, the relationship of Gospel and culture and of evangelism and social action, the priorities of mission and ministry and the style of training needed. The context in which we live shapes our thinking on so many issues. This is why those who are training to be Christian leaders need to be exposed to a variety of contexts; it is not enough to read about them. The problem is that it takes time to build up relationships to the point where people trust us enough to 'open up' and this is why college 'field placements' of a few weeks can never be fully satisfactory. In theory the part-time courses and TEE should be more effective because they enable the student to remain in his job, his social circle and in his local church. He is trained *in* ministry rather than *for* ministry and is able to relate what he learns to the context and culture where he lives. However, it has been found in practice that many of the students on courses experience difficulty in standing back from and reflecting on the world of their work, which in any case may be a limited one. The residential college may be as effective for such reflection. The TEE approach was valuable in the North of Argentina where Indian ordinands would have found it difficult both economically and psychologically to leave their remote villages in order to attend a residential college in a strange city. They would have had to give up their work, their homes, their culture and their way of life. But the particular disadvantage of TEE is that it may not provide the kind of cross-cultural experience where students are exposed to those from other cultures and are thus better able to recognise and reflect on the characteristics of their own.

The pros and cons of context and community experience can be expressed as a chart. A high level of community experience with a low level of exposure to context will result in intensity and ghettoism. The opposite 'corner'

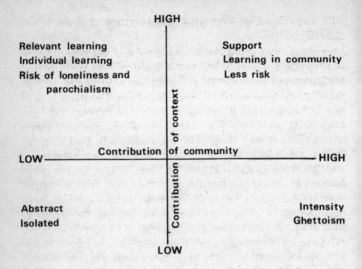

may mean learning that is relevant but it can also bring loneliness and parochialism.

The pattern of training that Jesus provided for the twelve combined experience of both context and community. They engaged in mission, but they also withdrew for quiet, reflection and prayer. The best pattern is one that combines both. A ministerial training course in the Midlands uses six week-ends a year for 'contextual' learning. Students make visits as a group to churches and work places in a variety of areas. A modified version of this pattern might be possible at local church level. One college gives its students a residential placement in an Urban Priority Area and another in a multi-faith district. A Baptist college in the North of England has experimented by basing its students in local congregations; they spend two and a half days a week in ministry within those congregations, two in university classes and one day in evaluation and reflection at college. The college then found that students became over-preoccupied with the affairs of the church and they have now supplemented the congregational placements with experience in community organisations outside the church.

A more radical suggestion is for students to spend a year in residential training, followed by one or two years' full or part-time practical ministry, followed again by a period of residential training. In a college in South India the first year is spent in college, followed by a second year spent in the city, either in a slum dwelling or in ordinary lodgings and often with a family of another faith. The third year includes a four months' placement and four months living in a community with a teacher available as a resource person. In Britain at any rate there are a host of practical problems with such a split, however ideal in theory. The average age of theological college students is higher than it used to be and a larger proportion are married with children; many wives are working. The family is therefore less mobile and the student may live out of college. This last factor must modify considerably what is said above about the values of community life in a residential college, and narrows the distinction between colleges and courses.

Whatever the detailed pattern the principles are to provide for both context and community experience and to see leadership development as a lifelong process. Both professional and non-professional leaders need special courses on moving to a new area, especially if the area is rural or inner city. Sabbatical and pre-retirement programmes are also vital. We need not a learned, but a learning leadership; it is all too easy to see final exams as a terminus rather than a staging post.

# APPENDIX: PRACTICAL PROJECTS

## A  A personal review for leaders

Ideally this personal review is a group exercise
– *on leadership style* (Chapter 4)
1. Try to discover the styles of leadership that are traditional
    in local industry, both in management and in unions,
    in local schools,
    in family life,
    in churches.
   What is the social and ethnic 'mix' of your area and do styles of leadership differ in the various social and ethnic groups?
2. Try to analyse your own style of leadership:
   Is it basically    traditional
                      charismatic
                      classical
                      human relations
                      systemic?
   What are its strengths and weaknesses?
3. What are your particular gifts? Are you basically:
       a teacher
       a pastor or counsellor
       an evangelist
       an organiser
       an administrator?
4. List the tasks you have to do and the areas where you have to give a lead.
   Does your style of leadership differ according to the task?

5. Ask these questions of others in leadership positions in your church.
– *on servant leadership* (Chapter 9)

How far are we ready to
    identify in our lifestyle with those around,
    be seen 'on the front line',
    admit mistakes,
    form close friendships while avoiding cliques,
    set an example in personal and family life,
    give direction without being domineering,
    account for our leadership?

– *on management of change and conflict* (Chapter 11)

1. What are our attitudes to change and why?

    Are we   over cautious
                   revolutionary
                   evolutionary?

2. What is our reaction to conflict and why?

    Do we normally   avoid
                                confront
                                coerce
                                compromise
        or work for        co-operation?

## B   Turned outwards to the world

A research project based on Chapter 8

1. *A Map*

Draw up a map of your area

Plot on it:  communications (road, rail, bus)
                churches, schools, colleges
                hospitals, clinics, social service centres
                police stations, council offices, public services
                shopping centres
                industrial and commercial work places
                major meeting places – post offices, community centres, youth clubs, pubs

               housing – different colours for council,
                  owner occupied, rented
Plot on it:   where your church members live
             where they work, if they work locally

You will need a different chart to show those working outside the local community.

2. *People*

Undertake research to discover the different kinds of people in the area.

Try to discover their attitudes to the area and their needs.

3. *Discover and discuss*

What are the main needs of the area?

What secular and church organisations are active in meeting these needs?

Which church members are involved in these organisations?

Are there new organisations or groups needed?

What support is needed for Christian leaders serving the local or the wider community?

4. *Education*

Plan a teaching programme to give Christian perspectives on local, national and global needs.

Plan opportunities for Christian leaders to share and discuss the issues they face at work and in society.

5. *An audit*

Encourage church members to undertake an audit on how much time they spend with family and Christian friends, with non-Christian neighbours, in church activities, and in service to the local community. Discuss the balance and be prepared to modify the church programme accordingly.

6. *A strategy*

Set goals and objectives for a mission strategy that includes both evangelism and social action.

There are a number of resource materials available to help in this kind of project. One written specifically for Urban Priority Areas that can be adapted for others is *An Audit for the Local Church*, available from Church House Book-shop, Great Smith Street, London, SW1P 3NZ.


## C   Goals and objectives (Chapter 10)

Plan a retreat or conference for your leaders.
Make sure there is adequate time for meditation, prayer and reflection.
Discuss –
   What is God calling us to do?
   Are we ready to move on and move out?
   Do we have the faith that God can provide and bless?
In the light of the above and of the research project based on Chapter 8 –
   Set out aims and objectives
   Plan how to communicate these aims and monitor progress


## D   Shared leadership (Chapter 5)

Ideally these questions are asked by each leader on his or her own, and then discussed with others.
1. What are the gaps in my leadership gifts and who can be found to fill those gaps?
2. Which of the tasks I do should be shared with or delegated to others? For the professional minister this might include:
   supervision of youth and Sunday school work
   marriage preparation
   baptism preparation
   counselling
   leading worship
   A deacon or church-warden will have a different list.
   A youth or housegroup leader will have a more limited and specific list.

3. Where these tasks are shared with others are they being shared in turn so as to avoid 'core group burn out'?
4. How much time is spent with other leaders – not only in discussion and planning, but in recreation, forming friendships, building relationships and in prayer?
5. Do our leaders represent a good 'mix' from the different social, age, intellectual and ethnic groups?
6. Is there a leadership team?
   If not, what steps can be taken to form one?
   If so, what steps can be taken to make it more effective –
     in open questioning and positive criticism,
     in mutual support and encouragement?

# E   Structures (Chapter 7)

1. Draw a structure map of the committees and organisations in your church.
   Draw lines of communication, liaison and accountability.
   Consult sample members of the congregation to discover whether they have understood the structures in this way.
2. Look at the list of other churches in the area.
   Do you know the leaders in those churches?
   How often do you meet?
   Are there tasks that can be done more effectively together?
   Is there a case for shared leadership, training and mission?
3. Discuss what action groups or committees are needed in the light of   community needs
                    goals and objectives
                    the traditions of your church
                    the leadership gifts and resources available
                    other churches and their resources
4. Discuss whether a central leadership group is needed and if so what its aims and composition should be:

should it be primarily for pastoral care, teaching, management or mission?

5. Discuss whether you ought to be a two-stage or three-stage church.

    Do you need sector leadership groups as well as a central one?

    Are the leadership groups there primarily to give support or direction?

6. Draw an ideal structure map, showing action groups and committees and including lines of communication, liaison and accountability.

# F   Delegation (Chapter 6)

1. Plan a regular opportunity to review the church membership list in order to identify the gifts of each member –

    to establish whether those gifts are being used and if not to create opportunities for their use.

2. Plan a regular review of the different aspects of church life and of the work of church members in the community –

    what are the present gaps?

    what understudy work needs to be done for gaps that are likely to appear in the near future?

    who can be approached, selected and trained for these gaps?

3. Discuss which of the tasks being undertaken need a job description. Begin a process of agreeing such descriptions.

4. Check what resources – financial, material and human support – are needed in each department of church life.

5. Work out a process of job discussion and evaluation.

    Decide   who needs it,

    who will undertake it,

    what process, written or verbal, should be used.

This review can be undertaken by a special group set up for the purpose, or by a permanent group, such as an elders' meeting, ministry committee, or a committee of staff and wardens or deacons. It can be undertaken annually, or a meeting can be held monthly or quarterly to look at certain aspects of church life and different sections of the membership list. Research can be undertaken by means of a questionnaire or by different members of the committee meeting with leaders of organisations.

## G   Development (Chapter 12)

1. Research and list the training and development materials available for church leaders, including those engaged in –
   Sunday schools
   youth work
   house groups
   adult organisations
   worship
   evangelism
   counselling
   community service
   the world of work
   Make a list of all such leaders.
2. Arrange a meeting of a central leadership group –
   this might be   the elders or deacons
                   the staff, wardens and readers
                   the standing committee
                   a group formed for the purpose
   Discuss
   (i) How far you yourselves are developing in leadership
       spiritually
       intellectually
       in practical skills
       in relationships

   (ii) How far other leaders are developing

  (iii) What courses ought to be planned or recommended

       in academic and biblical study

       in management, counselling or communication

       in other specialist skills

  (iv) Whether an individual or a group should be appointed to have oversight of leadership development and training

   (v) Whether there are others who should be trained for leadership.

3. Draw up a programme for training and development of leaders.

4. Check whether the development programmes you plan
    combine action and reflection,
    are in mission as well as in ministry,
    are in the world as well as in the church,
    include development in relationships and team building.

# NOTES

## 1 Dictator, bureaucrat or counsellor?

1. Max Weber, *The Theory of Social and Economic Organization.*
2. Kane, pp. 71 and 72.
3. Hendrix, p. 12.
4. Walker, p. 137.
5. Eddie Gibbs argues that the ship will not get very far if the captain spends all his time visiting the sick bay; Gibbs, p. 387.
6. Rudge, pp. 38–46.

## 2 Chieftain, patron, guru or executive?

1. Keeley, p. 159.
2. Sheppard, p. 286.
3. An example of this in the Mennonite Fellowship is described in a paper published by Administry in December 1986.
4. Wagner, *Leading Your Church to Growth*, p. 173.
5. Montgomery, p. 240.

## 3 Prophet, priest, king, elder

1. See, for example, *Understanding Christian Leadership* by John Eddison.
2. Stott (ed.), *Obeying Christ in a Changing World*, Vol. 2, p. 68.
3. At certain periods use was made of two objects called Urim and Thummim, kept in the high priest's robes. They may

have been gems or stones and may have been used in a form
of casting lots.

4 Warkentin, p. 165.
5 Lightfoot, pp. 95–9.
6 Harper, pp. 44–5.
7 Gibbs, p. 340.
8 The word is *diakonos*, translated 'servant' in the NIV and
'deaconess' in the RSV. Either translation is in theory possible, but the latter is more likely and in any case a 'servant of
the church' is likely to be an officer or leader. She is also
called a *prostatis* which can have the meaning of 'a woman set
over others'.
9 A fuller discussion of the issues in this chapter can be found in
Michael Green's *Freed to Serve*, Hodder & Stoughton
(1983).

## 4 Asking questions

1 Christian Leadership Letter, World Vision, May 1983.
2 Wagner, *Leading Your Church to Growth*, pp. 92–3.
3 Rudge, p. 132.
4 See also the discussion on p. 160.
5 Administry, page 11. I have taken the liberty of substituting
'organiser' and 'organising' for Dr Griffiths' original 'administrator' and 'administrative' in order to be consistent with
our working definition.
6 Tiller, p. 69.
7 A further illustration of this distinction between organising
and consultant leadership can be found in the modern matrix
method of management discussed on pp. 107–8.
8 RSV and NIV translate *kubernesis* as 'administrator' but by our
definition it might be better to use this word of the 'helpers'.
9 Prior, p. 68.
10 Administry, p. 12.

## 5 Shared leadership

1 *To a Rebellious House?*, p. 32.
2 Quoted by Bishop J. A. T. Robinson in *The New Reformation?*, p. 55.
3 Quoted Vogel, p. 22.

4   Sookhdeo, *Strategy for Urban Mission*, 'Mainstream' News-
    letter No. 14, September 1983, p. 4.
5   Watson, *I Believe in the Church*, pp. 352, 367.
6   Peters and Waterman, *In Search of Excellence*.
7   Peters and Waterman, p. 16.
8   Adair, p. 44.
9   Ortiz, p. 16.
10  Montgomery, p. 114.
11  Peters and Waterman, p. 323.
12  Parkinson, p. 112.
13  Laird, Chapter 2.
14  This was recognised in the Church of England report *Team
    and Group Ministries*, GS 660.
15  Administry, p. 12.

**6   Delegation**

1   Stott, *One People*, p. 66.
2   Study by Extension for All Nations, Allen Gardiner House,
    Pembury Road, Tunbridge Wells, Kent, TN2 3QU.
3   Adair, p. 136.
4   Laird, p. 7.
5   Sheppard, pp. 255, 256.
6   Described in D. James Kennedy, *Evangelism Explosion*,
    Coverdale (1970).
7   *Missionary Methods – St Paul's or Ours?*
8   Laird, Chapter 3.

**7   Renewing the structures**

1   Albert H. van den Heuval, *The Humiliation of the Church*,
    SCM Press (1966), p. 50; quoted Taylor, p. 121.
2   Administry, Resource Paper No. 82.4.
3   Beasley-Murray and Wilkinson, Chapter 7.
4   Quoted Townsend, p. 152.

## 8 Turned outward to the world

1  Webster, p. 28.
2  Snyder, *The Community of the King*, p. 48.
3  Anderson and Jones, p. 51.
4  Watson, *I Believe in the Church*, p. 306.
5  A useful discussion on the relationship of evangelism and social action can be found in The Willowbank Report, Lausanne Occasional Paper No. 2, published under the title *Explaining the Gospel in Today's World – Gospel and Culture*, Scripture Union (1978).
6  Wallis, pp. 9, 5, 6.
7  Snyder, *The Problem of Wineskins*, Chapter 4.
8  Quoted Eberhard Bethge, *Dietrich Bonhoeffer*, p. 446.
9  Fife and Glasser, pp. 104–5.
10  A useful study was produced by the World Council of Churches in 1968 called *The Church for Others*.
11  Greenway, p. 83.

## 9 Servant leadership

1  D'Epinay, p. 47.
2  Adair, p. 100.
3  Roy, p. 304.
4  Peters and Waterman, p. 289.
5  *Faith in the City*, p. 38.
6  Quoted Adair, p. 165.
7  Op. cit., p. 103.
8  Andrew Walker has provided a full documentation in his book *Restoring the Kingdom*. There is also a valuable discussion in Donald Bridge's book *Spare the Rod and Spoil the Church* (Chapter 10), MARC Europe (1985) and in Jeremy Barr's book *Freedom and Discipleship* (Chapter 3), IVP (1983).
9  Tiller and Birchall, p. 57.
10  Quoted Bax, p. 110.
11  Warren, p. 126.
12  Watson, *Fear No Evil*, p. 119.

## 10  The leader's vision

1   Harper, p. 50.
2   Beasley-Murray and Wilkinson, p. 16.
3   James Stewart, *A Man in Christ*, Hodder (1935), p. 318, quoted in David Sheppard, *Built as a City*, p. 354.
4   Tom Walker, p. 57.
5   Quoted Adair, p. 185.
6   Other practical examples can be found in *Listening to God* by Joyce Huggett, especially Chapters 9–13.
7   Adair, p. 79.
8   Taylor, p. 5.
9   Wagner, *Your Spiritual Gifts Can Help Your Church Grow*, p. 162.
10  Hendrix, p. 26.
11  Montgomery, pp. 10–11.

## 11  Change and conflict

1   Harris, p. 14.
2   Rudge, p. 113.
3   Tofler, *Future Shock*.
4   Harris, p. 43.
5   Stott, *Christ the Controversialist*, p. 52.
6   These are spelt out in *Discover your Conflict Management Style* by Speed B. Leas.
7   Huggett, pp. 10, 20.
8   Sanders, p. 32.
9   Harris, pp. 53, 86.
10  Verses 20 and 29 of Acts 15 present some difficulty and I have accepted Professor F. F. Bruce's suggestions. See F. F. Bruce, *The Book of the Acts*, Eerdmans (1954), pp. 311–12.

## 12  Leadership development

1   Green, p. 15.
2   It is heartening to see a revolutionary document produced by the Advisory Council for the Church's Ministry (ACCM) of the

Church of England called *Education for the Church's Ministry* (ACCM Occasional Paper No. 22, January 1987, obtainable from Church House, Westminster).

3   See the comments made by Tiller and Birchall on pp. 69 and 70 of *The Gospel Community*.

4   There are also a large range of development and training materials available from publishers, dioceses and voluntary societies and organisations.

5   Tiller and Birchall, p. 64.

6   The need for this is illustrated on p. 34.

7   ACCM Occasional Paper No. 22, quoted above, p. 29.

8   Anderson and Jones, p. 6.

9   From *Theological Education Today*, an address given by the Archbishop of Canterbury at Great St Mary's, Cambridge, 26 September 1986.

10  Webster, p. 23.

# BOOKS QUOTED

ADAIR, J., *Effective Leadership*, Pan Books (1983).

ADMINISTRY, Resource Paper No. 82.4 (28 Fontmill Close, St Albans, Herts).

ALLEN, R., *Missionary Methods – St Paul's or Ours?*, World Dominion Press (1960).

ANDERSON, J. and JONES, E., *The Management of Ministry*, Harper & Row (1978).

BAPTISM, EUCHARIST AND MINISTRY, The Lima Report, Faith and Order Paper No. 111, World Council of Churches, Geneva (1982).

BAX, J., *The Good Wine*, CIO (1986).

BEASLEY-MURRAY, P. and WILKINSON, A., *Turning the Tide*, Bible Society (1981).

BETHGE, E., *Dietrich Bonhoeffer*, Collins (1977).

D'EPINAY, C. L., *Haven of the Masses*, Lutterworth (1969).

EDDISON, J., *Understanding Christian Leadership*, Scripture Union (1974), reprinted 1983.

FAITH IN THE CITY, Church House Publishing (1985).

FIFE and GLASSER, *Missions in Crisis*, IVCF (1961).

GIBBS, E., *I Believe in Church Growth*, Hodder & Stoughton (1981).

GREEN, M., *The Meaning of Salvation*, Hodder & Stoughton (1965).

GREENWAY, R., *An Urban Strategy for Latin America*, Baker Book House (1973).

HARPER, M., *Let My People Grow*, Hodder & Stoughton (1977).

HARRIS, J. C., *Stress, Power and Ministry*, The Alban Institute (1977).

HENDRIX, O., *Management for the Christian Worker*, Quill Publications (1976).

HUGGETT, J., *Listening to God*, Hodder & Stoughton (1986).

KANE, A., *Let There Be Life*, Marshalls (1983).

KEELEY, R., *Christianity a World Faith*, Lion (1985).

LAIRD, D. A. and E. C., *The Techniques of Delegating*, McGraw-Hill (1957).

LEAS, S. B., *Discover Your Conflict Management Style*, The Alban Institute (1984).

LIGHTFOOT, J. B., *St Paul's Epistle to the Philippians*, Macmillan (1896).

MONTGOMERY, *The Path to Leadership*, Collins (1976).

ORTIZ, J. C., *Call to Discipleship*, Logos International (1975).

PARKINSON, C. N., *Parkinson's Law or the Pursuit of Progress*, John Murray (1957).

PETERS, T. J. and WATERMAN, R. H., *In Search of Excellence*, Harper & Row (1982).

PRIOR, D., *The Church in the Home*, Marshalls (1983).

ROBINSON, J. A. T., *The New Reformation?*, SCM Press (1965).

ROY, J., *The Battle of Dienbienphu*, Harper & Row (1965).

RUDGE, P. E., *Ministry and Management*, Tavistock Publications (1968).

SANDERS, J. O., *Men from God's School*, Marshall, Morgan & Scott (1965).

SHEPPARD, D., *Built as a City*, Hodder & Stoughton (1974).

SNYDER, H. A., *The Community of the King*, Inter-Varsity Press (1977).

SNYDER, H. A., *The Problem of Wineskins*, IVCF (1976).

STOTT, J., *Christ the Controversialist*, Tyndale Press (1970).

STOTT, J. (ed.), *Obeying Christ in a Changing World*, Collins (1977).

STOTT, J., *One People*, Falcon (1969).

TAYLOR, J. V., *The Go-Between God*, SCM Press (1972).

TEAM AND GROUP MINISTRIES, CIO, Published by General Synod (1985).

THE CHURCH FOR OTHERS, Two Reports on the Missionary Structure of the Congregation, World Council of Churches, Geneva (1968).

TILLER, J., *A Strategy for the Church's Ministry*, CIO (1983).

TILLER, J. and BIRCHALL, M., *The Gospel Community*, Marshall, Morgan & Scott (1987).

TO A REBELLIOUS HOUSE? CIO (1981).

TOFLER, A., *Future Shock*, Pan Books (1970).

TOWNSEND, R., *Up the Organisation*, Michael Joseph (1970).

VOGEL, P., *Go and Make Apprentices*, Kingsway (1986).

WAGNER, P., *Leading Your Church to Growth*, MARC Europe (1984).

WAGNER, P., *Your Spiritual Gifts Can Help Your Church Grow*, Glendale, California, Regal Books (1979).

WALKER, A., *Restoring the Kingdom*, Hodder & Stoughton (1985).

WALKER, T., *Renew Us By Your Spirit*, Hodder & Stoughton (1982).

WALLIS., J., *The Call to Conversion*, Lion (1981).

WARKENTIN, M., *Ordination – A Biblical-Historical View*, Eerdman (1982).

WARREN, M., *I Believe in the Great Commission*, Hodder & Stoughton (1976).

WATSON, D., *Fear No Evil.*, Hodder & Stoughton (1984).

WATSON, D., *I Believe in the Church*, Hodder & Stoughton (1978).

WEBER, M., *The Theory of Social and Economic Organization*, trans. A. M. Henderson and Talcott Parsons, ed. Talcott Parsons, Glencoe Illinois, The Free Press, Edinburgh (1947).

WEBSTER, D., *Not Ashamed*, Hodder & Stoughton (1970).